take 'em along

take 'em along

SHARING THE WILDERNESS WITH YOUR CHILDREN

BARBARA J. EUSER

CORDILLERA PRESS, INC.

Publishers in the Rockies

Copyright 1987 by Barbara J. Euser

Library of Congress Cataloging-in-Publication Data

Euser, Barbara J., 1949-
  Take 'em Along.

  Includes index.
  1. Outdoor recreation for children. 2. Backpacking.
I. Title. II. Title: Take them along.
GV191.63.E97   1987   796.5'088054   86-31908
ISBN: 0-917895-12-6

Cover photographs by Ron Ruhoff

Printed in the United States of America

ISBN: 0-917895-12-6

Cordillera Press, Inc.
P.O. Box 3699
Evergreen, Colorado 80439
(303) 670-3010

Contents

"You'd be laughing, too, if you got carried all the way up here."
Jung Family Photo.

Yes You Can!

The past few years have seen an explosion of interest in hiking, backpacking, cross-country skiing, and other wilderness activities. Many of us who engaged in these outdoor activities before we had children have now entered a new phase of our lives—one that includes the constant patter of little feet and the breathless questions of excited voices. Somehow, we must introduce our children to the wilderness activities we love and make whatever accommodations prove necessary. At times those accommodations may be extraordinary!

Those of us having our families in the 1980s may feel like pioneers embarking on the Oregon Trail when it comes to organizing a child's first backpacking trip. Be assured, however, that families have taken their children into the wilderness for decades and not only survived the experience, but relished it. Some of the families described in this book have children now in their twenties who have been backpacking since they were a few months old.

Each family's background and outdoor experience determine what sort of adventures it will be inclined to take with children. As a rule, families cut back the scope of their activities when they take their children along. But not everyone cuts back to the same degree. When a mountaineer who has climbed in the Himalayas reduces his or her activity to accommodate children, the result is a substantially more ambitious outing than one attempted by someone who has never camped out more than three nights in a row.

The adventures described in *Take 'em Along* come from families whose experience covers the entire spectrum of outdoor activity. Some of the children are now grown; others are still toddlers. Some families include two parents who have engaged in major climbing and skiing expeditions throughout the world; other families have only one adult with outdoor experience; and some families have parents whose experience is limited to short backpacking trips. These differing backgrounds have produced an interesting phenomenon: Children of any given age have widely varying capabilities in the outdoors, but those capabilities are more closely related to their parents' attitudes and experience than any other factor.

While writing this book, I learned that on many family excursions something happened that was especially memorable—be it funny, exciting, or difficult. On the majority of outings, however, nothing out of the ordinary happened at all. Adults and children alike simply enjoyed themselves hiking, skiing, or canoeing. In my estimation, that was the true sign of success—the outing wasn't a rare, once-in-a-lifetime event, nor was it something akin to Green Beret survival training. The key is that families became so accustomed to doing something together that it was the common, normal thing to do. The excursions that work so smoothly may not make the best additions to family story-telling lore, but they do indicate that through experience, family members achieve a certain comfort level while sharing the out-of-doors.

Over the years, each family mentioned in this book has learned a few tricks, and each has some favorite trip they remember. These stories and experiences demonstrate that it is not only possible, but indeed rewarding to parent and child alike, to be a parent and continue venturing outdoors.

The most important point of this book is that YOU CAN DO IT TOO! Even if your previous outdoor experiences are limited, you can begin by taking your child on a hike. It is wise to start with short, easy trips first, then, paying close attention to your child's interest and capabilities, gradually increase the difficulty and complexity of trips. *Take 'em Along* describes a wide range of hikes, backpacks, horsepacks, canoe trips, and bicycling adventures, all of which demonstrate that an excursion doesn't have to be difficult to be satisfying. *Take 'em Along* also shows that a trip need not be severely limited in difficulty or duration just because children are involved. It is important to recognize that if you are doing something you love, your children will respond to that and will begin to love the activity, too.

By including our children in the activities we enjoy—and frequently *need* for sanity's sake—not only are we able to continue enjoying the outdoors, but also we are making our children's lives richer by introducing them to a new environment and all the different experiences that involves. Children will think of new questions to ask about mountains, rocks, trees, and water. Parents will have the opportunity to demonstrate that even if they don't know all the answers, they, too, are curious about the wilderness. The whole family has an opportunity to search for the answers together.

Outings, particularly overnight trips, require cooperation among all participants. Parents may break out of their at-home roles and give their children a chance to see them in a new light. The new environment of the wilderness provides an unparalleled opportunity for learning on many different levels in many different ways.

To take advantage of the opportunities, there is only one requirement:Go ahead and try it! True, there is an extra effort required, but each time you go for a hike or a ski tour or an overnight backpack, you learn more about what to expect and you get better organized. Wilderness activities become easy, natural things for the whole family to do. We remember that there is a fascinating wilderness out there to explore.

Let's take our children along and rediscover it together!

"Brrrr. Thank goodness for hot chocolate and Cream of Wheat!"
McLeod Family Photo.

Chapter One

Backpacking

B ackpacking is the most complicated activity discussed in this book. Before you can go, you must be able to hike, and carrying all your camping equipment on your back is far more difficult than loading it onto a pack animal. So considering this most complex activity first will make cross-country skiing, horsepacking, canoeing, and hiking seem simple by comparison.

TROUT LAKE:
Making That Initial Effort

On a warm, mid-August weekend when my daughter Helane was two years and ten months old, I decided to take her on her first overnight backpacking trip. Dean—husband and father—was not inclined to go. So I packed one sleeping bag, two foam pads, a two-man bivouac tent, stove, pots and food, hats, gloves, sweaters, jackets, and a change of clothes for Helane. All this fit into a Lowe Alpine Systems expedition pack that left enough room for Helane to sit on top—barely.

As I put the pack and Helane into the car, Dean changed his mind. So Helane and I added Dean to the expedition—plus our two golden retrievers, Henry and Daisy. Dean brought

his own pack of gear, along with a pack for Henry to carry.
It was early afternoon when we left our home in Golden
Gate Canyon west of Denver and drove toward a lake I had
located on the map. The lake appeared to be approximately
two miles from the trailhead. By the time Dean repacked
various items at the parking lot and we started hiking, the
afternoon thundershower had passed. Helane walked for a
half mile, then insisted on being carried.

The trail ascended a ridge and then dropped down toward
our objective, Trout Lake. Climbing the ridge, we cut through
scattered willows. The walking was not difficult and the dogs
raced back and forth through the willows and the channels
beneath them. Then the sun disappeared behind the mountains above us as we topped the ridge and saw the valley
spread below.

Then, horrors! We discovered that Henry had lost his pack!
Bad enough to lose the pack itself, but what was inside? While
repacking in the parking lot, Dean had transferred our stove,
pots, and matches into Henry's pack. Our dinner plans were
not elegant: hot dogs (Helane's favorite), macaroni and
cheese, and hot chocolate. Nor was breakfast any better:
oatmeal, hot chocolate, and coffee. But without a pot, a stove,
and those most basic and indispensable items—matches—the
culinary prospects were grim.

We dropped our packs and searched for the missing pack.
But no luck. Finally, we had to decide either to press forward
and set up camp in the dark or else retreat. Having come as
far as we had, we decided to continue on and eventually
reached Trout Lake. In the dark we located a marginally flat
spot near the shore and pitched our tent by flashlight. For
dinner we sat on a rock and ate cheese, gorp, and cold hot
dogs.

But Helane was having a great adventure. The moon was
full, a stream of light reflected off the still water of the lake,
and a crispness in the air signalled the end of summer at
11,000 feet. We crowded into the tent and told stories until
late, then Dean moved out to enjoy less crowded conditions,
but he had forgotten his foam pad and ended up more uncomfortable than before. Helane, on the other hand, slept soundly.

"This here's a rock." *White Family Photo.*

Next morning, as the sun's fingers crept across the lake to our campsite, we emerged for a meager breakfast of an orange and some granola bars. But nothing bothered Helane. After this "meal," she and I, along with Henry and Daisy, explored our way around the shoreline as Dean attempted to capture in the warmth of the sun the sleep he had missed the night before. As we circled the lake, we located lovely campsites; we watched ducks glide in and out of the grasses; we examined flowers and mushrooms of innumerable varieties, sloshed through marshes, ran across meadows, peeked over hillocks, jumped across streams, and finally reached our campsite once again.

Then it was time to head home. We loaded up, Helane riding in the Lowe pack on Dean's back as far as the top of the ridge. There we stopped once again to search for Henry's pack in some tangled willows. Dean caught sight of it, retrieved it, and we enjoyed our midmorning oatmeal along with an expansive ridge-top view. Walking downhill along the trail was something Helane enjoyed, and as we exchanged stories, Helane wove the longest, most interesting stories she had ever told. We reached the parking lot with the conclusion that Helane's first backpacking trip—while not without its mishaps—had nevertheless been a great success.

That first experience taught us several lessons:

(1) Backpacking with a child, at least a short one-nighter, can be done almost spontaneously. It doesn't require much more planning than required for adults.

(2) The trip doesn't have to—and probably shouldn't—involve miles and miles of hiking to achieve a sense of wilderness. You can separate yourself from everyday home life when you've hiked far enough from the car that you can't return to it for that one desperately important item you forgot to bring along. Hiking a couple of miles makes a child, as well as many adults, feel as though they have entered a totally new environment, far removed from the everyday fare of television, electric lights, and running water. What is valuable is the sense of independence, of carrying everything you require yourself. And you can convey to children the freedom to move about unhampered by houses and cars.

(3) A short overnight trip is a good way to introduce a child to backpacking. On our first backpack with Helane we were away from home only twenty-four hours; yet, we traveled a long way when measured by memorable experiences.

(4) Having a clear objective for the trip helps define the experience. Hiking away from the car into the woods for a couple of hours may yield a nice woodsy campsite, but a

child responds more positively to the idea of a definite objective—it's much easier to know when you've gotten there. Lakes are excellent objectives.

(5) Taking a child's favorite foods along makes the backpacking experience seem less strange. Helane's favorites during the summer of our first backpack were hotdogs, macaroni and cheese, and oatmeal. It was easy to pack for our overnight since I had plenty of her favorites on hand. Kids generally have a favorite breakfast cereal; macaroni or spaghetti or rice are often kids' dinner choices as well as lightweight backpacking foods. My friend Dale Hayes, a dietician by profession, packs a bag full of peanut butter sandwiches for her son for backpacking trips. She is sure the monotony won't hurt him for a couple of days, and by taking his favorite food, she knows he'll have the energy required for hiking.

(6) Keep the "marginal" gear to a minimum. My tendency when camping is to pack too many clothes for myself and to do the same for Helane. Since the parent is going to be carrying an extra load under the best of circumstances, an easy and effective way to cut back on weight is to cut back on extra clothes. I assume Helane will fall in a stream, or more likely, sit down in a puddle, but one full change of clothes is all I take for her. For myself I don't take extras—just a sweater, jacket, hat, and gloves. It's not exactly *fastidious*, but it doesn't hurt to wear the same clothes for a couple of days.

Other than clothes, the only extra item I carried for Helane on our first backpack was a foam pad. She shared my sleeping bag. She was still small, and I anticipated that she would prefer to cuddle up with me rather than sleep in a separate bag. So I left her bag at home. A small child will also fit comfortably in between two parents whose bags zip together; this will eliminate the weight of an extra bag for at least a season or two. A down jacket can double as a child-sized sleeping bag. Another lightweight option is a down elephant's foot, a half-length bivouac bag designed to be used by an adult with a

"Press on men! Got to make camp by nightfall." *McLeod Family Photo.*

down jacket for the upper half. Most six- or seven-year-olds will fit comfortably into an elephant's foot.

Allowing a child some choice in equipment may prove beneficial. My friend Sue Ellen tells me that her daughter Brooke insisted on a bright purple sleeping bag and is so enamored with it that Brooke allows no one else to carry it!

One final piece of equipment—considered indispensable by some families—is a whistle. Attach it to a string and have the child wear it around his or her neck every waking moment—from getting up in the morning until tucked into the sleeping bag at night. As one mother pointed out to me, the very act of screaming for help wastes the energy a child should conserve if lost. Screaming for help also increases the feeling of panic that all people experience when lost. Rescuers can hear a whistle for a longer distance than a yell and the child can blow it many times while expending little energy. It is essential to teach the child to sit down immediately—some say "hug a tree"—and blow the whistle, if he or she loses sight of adults.

CHICAGO BASIN:
They're Never Too Young To Start, But Who Carries the Diapers?

Debi and Jerry Jung are avid hikers who took their son Eric on a three-night backpack into the Needles Mountains in Colorado when he was only eight months old. They took the narrow gauge train from Silverton to Durango, Colorado, and disembarked at Needleton. From there they hiked up the long

"No, silly! You're only supposed to blow your whistle if you get lost!" *Bunin Family Photo.*

and well-traveled trail to Chicago Basin. Eric had been born in December; so during that first summer he was easy to transport in a Gerry carrier, a cloth pack on an aluminum frame. But distributing the gear that had to be carried was—and is always—an issue. In this case, Debi carried Eric, diapers, and lightweight gear. Jerry carried a double load part way up the trail, then split things. He made one trip to the campsite, then returned for the rest of the load. The "rest of the load," however, included items not required on all backpacking trips—hard hats and additional gear that Debi and Jerry needed to climb several mountains notorious for rockfall. The next day Debi climbed Sunlight and Windom, two fourteen-thousand-foot peaks connected by a ridge, and Jerry took care of Eric. The following day Jerry climbed Mount Eolus while Debi looked after the baby. On the fourth day they hiked out to Needleton and caught the train back to civilization.

CIRQUE OF THE TOWERS:
Flexibility Is The Key

A couple of years ago Dale Hayes and her husband, Bill Bredehoft, took their family and a couple of friends on a three-day backpack into the Cirque of the Towers in the Wind River Mountains of Wyoming. Bill remembered the trail as being long and flat with one significant hill at the end before it dropped down to the lake at the base of the cirque. But when he hiked it with Dale, their two children, and a couple of friends, it seemed as if the trail had changed.

At the time, Patrick was five years old and Rebecca just six weeks old. Dale carried the baby in a Snugli, a cloth baby carrier worn in front, and put a modified Gerry carrier on her back. Sleeping bags and disposable diapers dangled from the Gerry carrier, which was to be used only as a backup in the case of a short-leg failure. Patrick carried a small pack that held his sweater, a book, and tiny trucks. Bill carried an extremely heavy pack containing tent, food, cooking gear,

"Looks like we're ready. Who's got the diapers?" *White Family Photo.*

"Mom, who else?" *White Family Photo.*

and clothes, as well as a rope and rock climbing gear. Their friends carried their own gear, but were unable to share any of the family's load.

Bill's memory of the long, flat trail was essentially correct. The critical difference was not the trail, but some of its inhabitants—hordes of buzzing mosquitoes in significantly greater numbers than on Bill's previous trip. Dale covered the baby's head with a scarf and the whole party kept moving because of the bites they suffered at every stop.

Young Patrick hiked the seven and one-half miles of flat trail with minimal difficulty, but when he reached the hill before the cirque, he stopped. The hill is otherwise known as Jackass Pass and has an elevation gain of over 2,000 feet in one mile! Dale suggested camping at the lake at the foot of the pass. Bill might have agreed, but he had his sights set on a rock climb in the cirque the next day. To camp short of the cirque would rule out his intended ascent.

So Dale packed Patrick into the Gerry carrier and with one child on the front and another on her back she slowly, steadily climbed up the pass—feeling that she qualified as its namesake. Near the top of the pass, she passed another lake— another potential campsite but for the climbing plans. Bill hiked behind with one of their friends whose new boots were doing serious foot damage.

At last Dale, the children, and the rest of the party arrived in the cirque, set up camp by the lake, and climbed into their oversized dome tents. Everyone fell asleep, exhausted. In the morning, after Bill and his climbing partner set out for their climb, Dale and Patrick intended to spend the day exploring the lakeshore, but the ferocious mosquitoes kept them confined to the tents. Their other friend also spent the day there. One woman read while her feet began to mend, and Dale envied her as she spent the day amusing the children in their oversized dome. Patrick had brought a couple of Matchbox trucks which kept him occupied. He and Rebecca made one short foray along the lake's edge to stretch their legs, but were quickly forced back inside by the buzzing mosquitoes.

Although the plan had been to spend two nights in the cirque, the one day spent in the tent was quite enough. Family and friends decided to hike out the next day. On their return, Patrick once again had to be carried up the pass, but he willingly hiked down it and proceeded to hike all but the last two miles to the trailhead. When I asked them whether their four-man dome tent was large enough to spend the day in, Dale responded with the rhetorical question, "Is *any* tent large enough to accommodate two children for an entire day?" Reflecting on the trip, however, Dale asserted that the only real problem was the time of year. July was apparently prime mosquito hatching time, at least in 1984. August or early September would have been a much better choice. Patrick was a strong young hiker, and had he been able to spend another day at the lake recuperating from the hike in, he probably could have hiked up the pass on the way out.

As it was, what enabled him to hike most of the way were the Two Feathers stories Dale and Bill wove for him. Dale invented Two Feathers, a little Indian girl whose life and adventures paralleled those of Patrick. Two Feathers lives out-of-doors, hikes a lot, and now has a baby brother.

Storytelling is a critical skill in hiking with young children. Two Feathers is an exciting character, but for those of us less imaginative than Dale, any long story will do. Storytelling is one of the unintended skills you develop when taking children into the wilderness.

When hiking with children, flexibility is critical. If any backpack trip begins to fall apart, it's extremely important to admit it (disappointing as it is) and revise your plans even if it means cutting everything short. Adding children to a group adds many factors that may require a change of plans. The mosquitoes in the Wind River Mountains would probably not have caused an adult party to hike out a day early, but two kids trapped in a tent all day long were enough to compel the group to change its plans. To do this gracefully may be the most difficult technique to learn when taking children along.

Backpacking with kids involves a constant balancing of their needs against the needs of the rest of the group. For Dale Hayes and Bill Bredehoft, it might have made sense to camp earlier on their hike into the cirque, but by doing that, the climbing plans of several members of the party would have been ruined. So the decision to fulfill the rock climbing goals of the adults prevailed over the children's need to stop hiking for the day. By the next evening, however, the balance had shifted; it became more important to cut short Dale's confinement in the tent with the kids than give the climbers an additional day of rock work. Dale had made an extraordinary effort to give her spouse a chance to climb; the next day it was his turn to be flexible.

As with any group, but particularly so with children, the needs of all members of the party must be considered, and sometimes that will require a change of plans. The important thing is not to get put out by the changes. It's not the changes that matter; rather it's the way they're handled that matters. A sour attitude about changing plans can spoil the atmosphere of the entire adventure.

SAN JUAN MOUNTAINS:
It's Doing It, Not The Distance That Counts

Trains like the Durango-Silverton narrow gauge line in southwestern Colorado are great assets to families who want to go camping in the wilderness. George and Reola McLeod used the train on a camping trip when their son Ian was only a few months old. On that trip they used the train as a substitute for backpacking. They had loaded their gear in backpacks, but when they got off the train at Elk Park, they hiked only a few hundred yards to a campsite in the aspen. The train enabled them to get away from roads, cars, and traffic without an arduous hike.

Later the same summer, the McLeods took Ian to the Needleton stop on the Durango-Silverton line for a weekend on the trail to Chicago Basin. This trip was more ambitious. When loaded up, George looked smaller than his backpack containing tent, sleeping bags, cooking gear, food, and who knows what piled high on top. George recalls how a woman passenger raised her eyebrows at the sight of Reola carrying Ian in a Gerry carrier with backpacks attached to both sides and another one underneath holding diapers and clothes. "Are you going for a long time?" she asked. To which George replied, "We've given up the city. We're going back to the wild. Our child can't make it in the smoggy atmosphere." The woman responded, "But what a wonderful idea!" George chuckled at his little deception all the way to camp about a mile up the trail.

George remembers it as a gorgeous weekend during which young Ian learned two things: cold and fire. Ian discovered that in the morning it was cold and he had to stay under the covers until mom or dad lit the fire. He also found out that the fire got rid of the cold, and that invariably put Ian in a good mood and made him laugh.

THE DESERT:
A Whole Different World

If you live in the West, the desert is a wonderful place to take children backpacking. There are so many great places to explore: Arches National Park, Canyonlands, Capitol Reef, Bryce Canyon, the Escalante River, and their related locales! Backpacking in the desert requires fewer clothes, thus lightening loads. The weather is very reliable, which means that the afternoon thunderstorms that you have to plan around in the mountains usually don't occur. The only desert-specific equipment required are good hats with visors, sunblock lotion, and a long-sleeved shirt and trousers (to wear in the event the sunblock was applied too late).

Late spring, before the snow has melted, but when the whole family needs to thaw out, is a perfect time for a trip to the desert. With luck, the cactus will be in bloom and the streams will have a little water in them.

Friends of mine, the Martins, have made frequent pilgrimages to the Utah desert ever since their two sons were very small. The sites of their excursions have been the various side

"Hi ho, hi ho, it's off to camp we go!" Canyonlands. *McLeod Family Photo.*

canyons of the Escalante River. There, as in so many desert canyons, the streams are intermittent, even in the spring. Water fascinates children, and when hiking through desert canyons, the water is too little to pose any great danger. The shallow pools and the tiny trickles meandering down the sandstone shelves make the hiking go much faster. It becomes a roving game of following the streambed, alternately splashing along then searching for the next set of puddles. And there is nothing more delightful than camping underneath a sandstone shelf next to a shallow pool on a clear, moonlit, desert night.

The weight of equipment plus children is a difficult problem to solve anytime, but desert camping provides a partial solution: Lighter sleeping bags are adequate for the warmer nights, you don't need a tent, and clothing is less in amount and lighter in weight. You will need to carry extra water throughout the day, however, and finding campsites with a water supply is, of course, obligatory.

You also need to remain aware of snakes and scorpions. Shake out your clothes and shoes in the morning to prevent surprise encounters with scorpions. Keep an eye peeled for rattlesnakes, but if there are any about, they will not be interested in surprises and will give plenty of warning of their

"What do you mean you haven't got anything on?"
McLeod Family Photo.

whereabouts. They have no desire to attack anything much larger than a mouse and will be grateful if you stay far enough away to allow them a graceful retreat.

The desert may not be the first place that comes to mind for an exciting backpacking adventure, but the beauty of the desert is more subtle than that of the mountains. That may be reason enough to introduce children to the unique pleasures of camping in these arid climes.

GROUP FAMILY CAMPING:
The More the Merrier

If your family knows another you think you would enjoy camping with—try it! There are many advantages to this approach. One of the most important is that child care responsibilities can be shared among all the adults. Typically, everyone packs in to a base camp located fairly close to the trailhead. An ideal site is one in the middle of a good climbing area so that various combinations of adults can ascend the peaks on their climbing days, then watch the kids on their rest day.

One memorable family camp of this type took place on the shores of Redfish Lake in the Sawtooth Mountains of Idaho a few years ago. Four families with children ranging from five months to sixteen years in age camped and climbed together for two weeks. The "backpack" portion of the trip was accomplished via a boat trip across Redfish Lake. Once the base camp was established, everyone took turns climbing and babysitting. Kids who could only climb small hills did just that, while parents carried children too young too walk, or just enjoyed the campsite. One family had brought along an unrelated teenager as a babysitter, who also managed to do some climbing. Some of the more ambitious ascents required the climbers to stay away from the base camp for one or two nights, but there were also summits within one day's reach. The camp on Redfish Lake also offered difficult rock climbs,

Up the ladder in canyon country. *McLeod Family Photo.*

"Ya make me nervous when ya watch me like that!" *McLeod Family Photo.*

excellent hiking and running trails, and good swimming. One member of the party remembers that someone carried a piece of special equipment—a mosquito netting tent that was used just for the five-month-old member of the group. Mosquitoes can make everyone quite miserable, but they are especially ferocious in attacking young children who don't know how to defend themselves. A lightweight mosquito netting tent may make the difference between a successful outing and one that ends in frustration for all members of the party.

Taking the boat across Redfish Lake had an effect similar to taking the Durango-Silverton train; the party used transportation as a substitute for hiking to get away from civilization. There are many other opportunities to increase your sense of being in the wilderness while minimizing the effort required to get there. When planning a trip, consider using a boat to cross to an otherwise inaccessible shore of a lake. Also consider trains which run through mountains or canyons. Still another alternative to carrying everything on your own back is to use a burro, llama, or horse (see Chapter Four).

OTHER THINGS TO KEEP IN MIND

Generally speaking, the easiest time to backpack with a baby is when the child is very small. Babies don't weigh too much, they sleep a lot, and if they are breastfeeding, there are no special food considerations. Babies can also sleep in their parents' sleeping bag. If the baby is too active for that, however, a down jacket can be substituted for a sleeping bag.

One item of crucial interest to all campers with children who are not yet toilet-trained is what do you do about diapers? Every family's solution is different. On the Wind River trip, Dale Hayes took disposable diapers and burned them. A bad idea! Although the diapers eventually burned, the black, acrid smoke was so offensive that on subsequent trips she decided to lay the diapers out to dry, then pack them out with the

"Ah, nothing like a little rest to cool off a bit." *McLeod Family Photo.*

rest of the garbage.

On their trip to Chicago Basin, Debi and Jerry Jung figured out the number of cloth diapers that Eric would use, added a couple for emergencies, then packed them in. Debi had no intention of washing the diapers while camping, but simply intended to dry them as much as possible then carry them out to be washed at home.

For desert trips, Barbara Martin went to a garage sale where she bought a number of single thickness diapers—the kind you have to fold yourself. As necessary, she washed the diapers out, then attached them to her pack, which made a strange sight. As she skimmed along over the sand, she looked like a ship under full sail. The diapers dried almost instantly in the sun and breeze, and she avoided the unpleasantness and extra weight of carrying out dirty, disposable diapers.

A difficult transition occurs when a family goes from one child to two. It is physically impossible for most parents to carry two children plus all the food and equipment required for four persons. So following the birth of a second child, most families wait to backpack until the older child can walk some distance. Happily, a backpacking trip doesn't have to involve a long hike to establish the sensations of mobility and independence. Walking a couple of miles to a lake, for example, is possible for some three- or four-year-olds to accomplish without assistance. That, in turn, makes it feasible for the family to backpack there.

There are different philosophies about what is appropriate for a child to carry on a backpacking trip. Some parents feel that the child is more a part of the group if he or she carries at least a daypack with personal gear—a sweater, snacks, and a couple of toys. Others think that the advantage of being a child is not having to carry anything at all and thus be completely free to run up and down the trail, make side excursions, climb on a log or rock, examine a flower or tree, and otherwise make the way amusing. The other side of the coin is that carrying a pack increases the child's sense of independence by carrying his or her own load and increases his or her sense of identification with the group.

In any situation, however, remain sensitive to the needs of each individual child. A hard and fast rule is the least effective way to deal with any situation. Flexibility is the key!

Water can be a problem. Unless you have access to water from a known source, such as the kitchen tap, on overnight trips you will have to treat all the water you use for cooking, drinking, and brushing teeth. This must be done to kill *giardia* cysts and other organisms. Years ago it was possible to drink from clear mountain streams without fearing the consequences, but that is no longer the case. You can boil the water for ten to fifteen minutes to purify it, or use chemical tablets or iodine drops. The easiest method is to drop the prescribed number of tiny tablets into a water bottle sometime well before the water is to be used. Chemical tablets are available at drugstores and mountaineering stores. Several small water filters are also on the market. The discomforts—stomach

"Almost like being in the shower at home." *McLeod Family Photo.*

cramps and diarrhea sometimes lasting for weeks—that result from carelessness in treating drinking water are just too unpleasant to chance.

Any time you plan a multi-day trip, it is important to consider what to do in case of emergency. Of course, you will take all precautions necessary to make sure that children don't fall into campfires or off cliffs, but despite the best precautions, accidents can occur. A major difference between first aid administered in town versus first aid administered in the wilderness is that medical attention is only minutes away in town, but many hours or even days away in the wilderness.

It is imperative to have a basic knowledge of first aid if you decide to attempt anything more ambitious than short day hikes. Give some thought to hypothetical situations when planning a trip. What if an accident happened at our third campsite? What is the quickest way out to a road? How long would it take to hike there? Where is the nearest doctor? Where is the nearest hospital? If one of the adults is injured and can't be carried out, how will we contact a local mountain rescue group?

A basic first aid kit will give you the confidence to deal with the minor problems that sometimes develop. Band-aids are ever popular with children and may ease minor cuts or scrapes. More important is soap to clean out superficial wounds. Adhesive tape, gauze pads, aspirin or aspirin substitutes, moleskin, an ace bandage (useful for holding a stick in place as a splint, if necessary), antibiotic cream, tweezers, a needle for dislodging splinters, insect repellent, and sunblock should also be included. In all likelihood, a skinned knee or a blister will be the extent of injuries sustained, but as the Girl Scouts and Boy Scouts have been taught for decades, it's always wise to "Be prepared."

OBSERVATIONS:
And Some Helpful Hints

When backpacking with children, keep the following points in mind:

(1) Plan a route with a definite objective, such as a lake, for the campsite.

(2) Plan a trip well within the capabilities of all the children and adults participating.

(3) Include the children's favorite foods in the menus.

(4) Pare down equipment to the absolute essentials to avoid excessively heavy packs.

(5) Make sure children wear whistles.

(6) Use alternative means of transportation such as boats

or trains to maximize wilderness experience and minimize carrying loads.

(7) Keep some long-winded stories in mind.

(8) Develop a plan of what you will do in case of emergency.

(9) Always treat the water you drink.

(10) Be flexible and have fun!

"Stretch and glide; stretch and glide." *James E. Fell, Jr. Photo.*

Chapter Two

Cross-Country Skiing

O ur first outdoor adventure with our daughter Helane was cross-country skiing. She was born on October 23, and by the time the New Year rolled around she found herself in a Snugli front carrier swaddled in layers of clothes for a ski trip up Jones Pass, west of Denver.

We had no guidance for this first excursion other than our common sense. Experience proved a more useful guide. We dressed Helane in a long-sleeved undershirt, socks, and her warmest sleeper, and completed her outfit with a hooded sweater. Then we zipped her into the Snugli; she was so tiny, however, that I had to stuff a blanket in with her to fill out the empty spaces.

Then I buckled and tied her onto Dean's chest, and helped him into his skis. It was snowing and not particularly pleasant out, but neither was it uncomfortably cold. Helane whimpered a little at first, then fell asleep.

After an hour of moderate uphill travel, we decided to turn around. The descent was naturally much quicker than the ascent, and that created problems. Dean was unaccustomed to his new weight in front—the closest he would come to experiencing my condition of recent months! Though an extremely competent skier, he soon found himself out of control and plunged forward into a snowbank. With some difficulty, I managed to pull him out and onto his feet. By then, Helane was wide awake and howling. We brushed the snow off the Snugli, while the bundle inside it wiggled and squirmed. Helane was essentially buried in the blanket inside the Snugli and she actually hadn't gotten any snow on her, but listening to her, you would have thought differently. Dean skied cautiously the rest of the way to the car, acutely aware of the screaming bundle attached to him.

"So this is what it's like being pregnant." Father Dean Crowell. *Euser-Crowell Family Photo.*

Barb, Dean, and three-month-old Helane.
Euser-Crowell Family Photo.

It took nearly forever to reach the car and get Helane inside. Only then did we discover that snow had gotten into the Snugli through the arm and leg holes. Then, when I unwrapped her, I discovered the real reason Helane was screaming. Neither fright nor cold, but a massive poop! Disposable diapers, disposable baby wipes, and a plastic bag in which to dispose of everything solved the problem. Once rediapered and clothed in clean sleepers, Helane nursed and fell asleep as though skiing was no great adventure at all.

As a result of our first ski trip, I made some improvements to our system. For future trips I decided to put socks on Helane's hands to provide more warmth; I cut holes in a waterproof stuff sack so that the Snugli could be put inside before it was strapped on; and I sewed the leg and arm holes in the Snugli's outer layer closed.

Those adjustments did the trick! During Helane's first winter we took a number of very enjoyable cross-country trips. From Montezuma to the pass above Saints John in central Colorado was a particularly nice one. The weather that day was quite pleasant. As usual, Helane slept during the entire ski, except when Dean stopped for a bite of lunch. Then she woke up crying. The motion of skiing is an excellent way to rock a baby to sleep, but the person carrying the child must have great stamina. In all likelihood, he or she will not be allowed to rest for the entire trip.

On a weekend trip to Vail, Dean did some downhill skiing while I took Helane ski-touring. Saturday we went to Meadow Mountain and skied back through the open glades, lunching in the barn of an abandoned ranch. The day was so warm that I took Helane out of the Snugli to bask in the sunshine.

On Sunday we skied up the road at Red Mountain. Unfortunately, for most of the trip we were on a route used by the local snow mobile concession, and though I always felt confident of help in case of emergency, the skiing was neither quiet nor serene.

The greatest challenge of these solo excursions was getting into my skis after I put on the Snugli and Helane. Maintaining my balance while bending over far enough to fasten my bindings was always a trick.

Although I always carried an extra diaper and baby wipes on these trips, I never changed Helane's diaper "in the field." The reason was that even on the warmest days, it was never warm enough to undress her as much as required to make the change. Instead, I always put a fresh diaper on her in the car before we started out, then figured that the clothes and blankets surrounding her would keep her warm, even if she wasn't dry. The diaper liners now available extend a diaper's life, and thus the potential length of a day trip.

Helane's longest ski trip during her first season was over Shrine Pass, just east of Vail. It involved four hours of skiing. The winds were fierce near the top of the pass that day, so we snapped a down vest around the stuff sack that enclosed the Snugli and tied a Gore-Tex parka around the entire bundle. Helane remained unaware of the cold.

One thing we learned that first season is that it's imperative to keep the entire child warm while skiing. With a tiny baby, you can do this easily with arrangements like the Snugli-stuff sack we devised. During all of our ski trips Helane herself was rarely seen. Occasionally, we dug down into the bundle to make sure she was breathing because she was almost completely buried in blankets. That was all by design, because we'd heard of a child whose eyes were damaged by exposure to the cold when her parents took her ski touring.

In addition to the obvious hazard of cold, there is the danger of excessive exposure to sun. Some of the nicest times to ski with children are those wonderfully warm, sunny days of spring. But they can be deceiving. The tender young skin of babies is extremely vulnerable to sunburn, and young eyes can be easily damaged by the intensely bright light reflecting off the snow. As a precaution against sunburn, use a good sunblock—the highest rated are none too strong. One couple whose children have extremely sensitive skin recommends Piz Buin, an imported sunblock that, though expensive, doesn't irritate children's skin, is very effective, and goes a long way.

As for eye protection, wide-brimmed hats that tie on provide some shade. Junior-size baseball caps work well if you sew on an elastic chinstrap. It is also better to use a hat than a visor to insure that the baby's scalp is protected from the sun. You can get child-size ski goggles at downhill ski equipment shops. And you can easily find sunglasses in junior sizes and secure them by elastic or neoprene bands such as croakies.

In some areas you may be concerned about altitude, but during our numerous ski trips in the Rocky Mountains with Helane we never encountered any altitude problems. Because we carried her, she did not exert herself at altitude and apparently never suffered any adverse effects. Each child is different, however. I know of one case in which a family took a baby only a few months old skiing and went to an elevation of around 11,400 feet. When they peered down into the Snugli to check him, although he was warm enough, his skin appeared

"Which way to the slopes?" *White Family Photo.*

quite gray. They immediately skied back to their car and drove to the nearest medical center, where a doctor told them that the baby's skin color was due to the diminished oxygen at that altitude. The couple was unable to determine any long-term adverse effects of the experience on their child, but it was upsetting at the time and a strong caution for future excursions.

Helane's second season of skiing was more of a challenge. At a little over a year, she was too heavy to be carried in a Snugli. The Gerry carrier, while fine for summer use, provided neither the protection from the cold which Helane required nor the suspension system to make carrying her reasonably comfortable.

Thus we devised another hybrid arrangement. Helane sat in the Gerry carrier inside a quilted bag with legs (made by Baby Bag), then we set the Gerry carrier into a Lowe Alpine

System expedition pack. The pack was one we had used for years in climbing. It had an interior frame of fiberglass stays, and the suspension system was designed for comfort when carrying loads several times the weight of a year-old child. We stuffed blankets into the pack to keep Helane's feet warm and provide extra insulation. The drawstring at the top of the pack made it possible to enclose her completely when necessary.

At one year Helane was much more aware of and interested in her surroundings than she had been the year before. She spent much more time with her head up looking around and much less time fast asleep. During lunch stops she insisted on getting out of the pack and moving around. We usually took a poncho or ground cloth to spread out during lunch stops to provide something for Helane to play on, as well as something dry for ourselves to sit on. We took our favorite one-day ski trips. From the time we left the car to our return was usually no more than four or five hours. It is hard to say how much Helane affected our skiing when she was one year old, although we may have unconsciously lowered our expectations. For longer trips, we arranged to leave her with my parents and we did not attempt to take her either snow-camping or staying overnight at a hut.

When Helane reached her third winter, we realized that she was too heavy to carry comfortably. I was also pregnant with our second child, and the combination made for a very limited number of ski trips. On one memorable day, however, we skied the Government Trail from Buttermilk to Snowmass, Colorado, with another couple—Candy and Ken—and their two-year-old son Brady. Both Candy and I were due to have babies the first of June. Dean carried Helane in the Gerry carrier inside the Lowe pack; Ken carried Brady in a Gerry carrier; Candy and I carried our babies inside. From the outset it was obvious that all the children affected our balance and speed as a party.

We anticipated we would be out for something longer than the two and one-half hours it had taken us to ski the Government Trail without children the year before. But we were still wrong. It took us *much* longer than anticipated. The weather deteriorated and a wet snow began to fall as the afternoon wore on. Helane was warm enough, but Brady began to get cold. We tied extra shirts and jackets around him to keep the snow off. On the Government Trail there is no easy way out, and the only thing to do was keep going. We finally reached the Snowmass ski area and took the children inside a lodge to warm up while we waited for a bus to take us back to the Buttermilk ski area. Unfortunately, we hadn't obtained complete information on the bus schedules before our trip, and we had missed the last free bus to Buttermilk. The buses also run much less frequently in the late afternoon; when we realized we would have had to wait for nearly an hour for the next one, we ended up taking a taxi back to Buttermilk. A very reasonable ski trip had turned into a long, hard day for the six (eight?) of us.

Our last cross-country trip that season was up Deer Creek from Montezuma with friends from Boston. The altitude slowed down our friends from sea level, my additional front load hindered my progress, and Dean labored under Helane's nearly forty pounds. We toured until we were all tired, then returned to the Montezuma Inn for hot cider and pastries.

That trip was a turning point for us. Dean decided that he could not carry Helane in the backpack again. At the advanced age of three and a half years, she had enjoyed her last ski on someone else's back.

Toboggans have eased many backs during the ski touring season. There are a number of different manufacturers and styles available. A lightweight toboggan can be much easier to use than a backpack because your upper body is free to extend, therefore one's skiing technique doesn't become cramped. The difficulties with toboggans, however, are their weight, cumbersome length, and their difficulty of remaining on track behind the skier. Because toboggans tend to slide down the fall line if the skier is on an incline, traversing a slope is especially difficult and sometimes dangerous. You may want to have a second adult with a rope tied to the tail of the toboggan to help keep it on track, or at least keep it from sliding away down the slope.

My friends Hans and Katie Wiggins have taken the toboggan

"Yes, folks, I really *can* breathe down here in this bundle." Near Aspen, Colorado. *Krebs Family Photo.*

alternative one step further. They have their well-trained golden labrador retriever pull their two children along!

The easiest place to ski with a toboggan is on a flat, well-packed track. Old railroad grades are ideal. One excellent spot is Boreas Pass outside of Breckenridge, Colorado. The railroad tracks were pulled out years ago and the roadbed that remains is a wide, easy, consistent grade running thirty-five miles over the mountains to Como. The upper part of the pass road is at timberline and is very exposed to the weather, but at lower elevations the road runs through trees and is reasonably well protected. At the old water tank on the Breckenridge side of the pass, about three miles from Highway 9, there are picnic tables among the trees—an excellent lunch spot.

Since toboggans are quite expensive to purchase—in the $150 to $225 range—it may not be feasible for one family to

"Not a bad way to travel, is it?" *Griffith Family Photo.*

buy one for a limited excursion. Two or three families can buy one together, however, or they may be rented at some cross-country ski areas. One toboggan model is built and sold commercially by John and Jini Griffith. It is designed to be used in tracks and has been very popular with cross-country ski areas which rent the units to families using their trails for a day.

The Griffith's toboggan comes equipped with safety straps for children, and that's important! On one occasion while testing a prototype of their toboggan, John Griffith was in the lead pulling one-year-old Erin as a guinea pig. Jini was a few minutes behind and when she skied around a corner, she discovered Erin crawling toward her down the ski trail. Erin had rolled out while turning a corner and John hadn't known it! He maintains he was concentrating on his technique at the time! Needless to say, Erin has been completely strapped in on all subsequent occasions.

Strapping children into a toboggan is important, especially when the toboggan will be going up or down hills. If it slides out of the ski track, it may dump the kids out in the snow. That may be fun, but not on a hillside where they could slide a long way. The age of four is a difficult time for skiing with children. They are too heavy to be carried in a pack, too impatient to be confined in a toboggan, and not coordinated enough to ski using poles, which are essential in cross-country skiing. At that age some parents have given up cross-country for a season or two and gone downhill skiing instead. There children are taught to ski without poles—gravity takes their place—and riding the lifts is an unparalleled thrill.

Take the case of my friends Sue Ellen Harrison and Michael McCarthy. They often skied cross-country when they could carry their daughter Brooke. By the time their son Fenton was born, however, Brooke was too big to carry. She could cross-country ski short distances if they found equipment for her; but Fenton got too heavy to carry. So their solution was to choose downhill skiing for a few seasons. As a bonus, they found that some areas let small children ski free or at least have short day discounts for children who usually can't ski all day. Following the birth of our second daughter, Piper, and our realization that four-year-old Helane was simply too heavy to carry, we have followed the lead of Michael and Sue Ellen. Dean and Helane downhill ski for the afternoon while I take Piper cross-country skiing, carrying her in the front Snugli. At the Lake Eldora area in Colorado, I have purchased a ticket for five dollars to ski on the groomed cross-country trails—a pleasant way to spend the afternoon. I have also crossed the ski area (at no charge) to gain access to the forest service trails which lead to the Gwyn Mountain Ski Hut and the Jenny Creek Trail. I have yet to explore either of those trails fully before I have had to return to the ski area to meet Dean and Helane when their half day is done.

Having taken Piper skiing a number of times, I have come to realize that it's definitely easier the second time around. Piper was four months older than Helane was during her first winter season, so Piper seemed less fragile. I think the main

"One little Piper." Barb Euser and daughter number two. *Euser-Crowell Family Photo.*

difference, however, was experience. Having skied many times with Helane, the novelty wore off. It wasn't anything new or particularly adventuresome. It was simply the way you ski when you have a seven-month-old baby. Every weekend presents a new challenge in finding ways to get out and ski. Recently Helane, Piper, and I drove with our friend Mary to a cabin near Breckenridge, Colorado. On Saturday I enrolled Helane in an all-day ski lesson at the nursery/ski school. That left Mary and Piper and me free to ski cross-country. We chose the French Gulch Trail and skied up to the top of the pass where it was too windy to do anything besides gulp down a few bites of food. We skied back down to the trees for a leisurely lunch in the sun. On our way back to the car we detoured to ski up to the head of Little French Gulch. By the time we returned to the car, Mary and I felt we had had a good day's skiing. Piper seemed content, and, when I picked Helane up from the ski school, it was clear she had had a good day's skiing, too.

The next day was even more interesting, though not from a wilderness perspective. Mary and her husband Michael, along with Dean, Helane, and I all bought downhill tickets. After Piper went to the ski area nursery, Dean and Helane skied on downhill equipment, and Mary, Michael, and I skied on cross-country equipment, working hard all day to perfect our telemark turns. We were able to telemark down the slopes Helane was able to ski with her wedge technique. By combining different equipment and techniques, we were able to ski together and at the same time challenge each of us. Perhaps that's what it's all about.

There is a reward for making the effort to introduce children to skiing at an early age. My friend George McLeod recalls the "little toy skis with rubber bands on them" that he and Reola purchased for their son Ian. George would clamp Ian's shoes into the skis and trundle along with Ian between his legs. George speaks for all parents when he says: "Nobody really enjoys doing that." But he is convinced that as a result of the early positive experiences of skiing first in a Gerry carrier on Reola's back, then on the "toy skis" between

"Don't take that last raisin; it's mine!" *McLeod Family Photo.*

George's legs, Ian now is the one asking George, "Can we go cross-country skiing?"

OBSERVATIONS:
And Some Helpful Hints

When cross-country skiing with children, try to keep the following points in mind:

(1) Protect your children from the cold. Make sure you have enough clothing, blankets, quilted bags, and other gear to keep your child warm. Socks make excellent mittens and several layers of hats are recommended.

(2) Protect your children from the sun. Use plenty of

"When I said keep your tips up, I didn't mean that far!" *White Family Photo.*

sunblock and wide-brimmed hats and either goggles or sunglasses to protect their eyes.

(3) Devise a system for carrying your child that isn't too painful for the adult to manage. I used a Snugli front carrier until Piper was eight months old, then switched to a Gerry carrier. For our older daughter, we used a Gerry carrier fitted inside a Lowe Alpine Systems pack to take advantage of its superior suspension system.

(4) Take along a poncho or tarp to spread on the snow during lunch stops so the child can get out and stretch a bit.

(5) Plan your ski trip keeping in mind that the person carrying the child is not going to be allowed to fall. This may mean choosing tours without steep downhill sections or realizing that the person who carries the child may need to side-step down some portions of the trail.

(6) Don't make the ski trips too long. Both parents and kids wear out earlier than adults without children.

(7) If you use a toboggan, strap the kids in, try to avoid steep slopes, and have an adult skiing behind.

(8) If at all possible, plan to end the ski trip at a lodge or inn where everyone can relax, warm up, and get something to eat and drink.

"Sometimes you're so tired after a day on the trail that you can go to sleep standing up. *Martin Family Photo.*

Chapter Three

Hiking

Hiking is the easiest wilderness activity to enjoy with children. You can find excellent trails almost anywhere. The only special equipment required is a Snugli or other front carrier for an infant, or a Gerry carrier for a toddler. Older kids will need adequate rain gear because they no longer fit underneath your parka or poncho. Tennis shoes are adequate foot gear for young hikers, so long as you do relatively short hikes where there isn't any snow.

A good hike for children should have the following characteristics:

(1) A significant objective such as a lake, an overlook, or a mountain top within an attainable distance.

(2) Limited elevation gain. Anything more than about five hundred feet vertical rise per mile seems very steep to young hikers. (And sometimes to parents!)

(3) Varied terrain that might include such things as meadows, streams, even switchbacks. A flat trail through uninterrupted forest is not too interesting for young "explorers."

The key to hiking with children, however, is the objective.

In all likelihood, children will not want to hike further just for the joy of hiking, so the objective must be a satisfactory end to the hike for everyone involved. In my family's experience, the most attractive destination is a lake within two or three miles of the trailhead.

FOREST LAKE:
Experiences Long-Remembered

When Helane was two and a half years old, she and I took a delightful hike to Forest Lake. We dropped Dean and a friend off to do some fishing in a privately owned stretch of water west of Rollinsville, Colorado, then drove to the east end of the Moffat Tunnel where we parked the car. Helane insisted on being carried from the outset, so it was fortunate that our objective was only two miles away. We carefully crossed the train tracks, climbed over the steel gate, then hiked along the road which turned into a trail just beyond the few private cabins.

The trail was full of interest as it passed crumbling and decaying cabins and was crossed by a number of streamlets. At the fork where we turned right to Forest Lake, we passed through an old townsite, a thriving community in the late 1800s, but now a barely distinguishable ruin among the wildflowers and grasses. We followed a wide trail up to a major stream crossing, during which Helane assisted by helping hold onto my boots while I waded through the freezing water. There were no other hikers to be seen, and the grade was gentle enough to allow us some enthusiastic singing. I lost the trail on the steep, final ascent to Forest Lake by crossing the stream unnecessarily. Helane fell asleep, and I labored up through a field of exquisite wildflowers in silence. Eventually I relocated the stream and the trail. We encountered several parties of hikers close to the lake. An excellent flat rock at the edge of the water provided our picnic spot. Helane awoke as I swung her down off my back and we soaked our feet and enjoyed our lunch before heading back down.

Helane, twelve-day-old Piper, and Mom on Piper's first hike. Hermann Lake, Colorado. *Euser-Crowell Family Photo.*

The way back provided more opportunity for singing and general conversation. I managed the one significant stream crossing without removing my boots—and without getting wet—but the rain started falling when we were about three-quarters of a mile from the car. I pulled the hood of my jacket over my head, held onto the sleeves, and spread the rest of it over Helane. As I made my way along the trail as quickly as possible, she fell asleep again. When we reached the car, we were damp and tired, but both of us had enjoyed a very good hike.

The value of a shared experience, such as a hike, often goes far beyond the time spent on the hike itself. For my family the value of a hike increases immeasurably as the experience is turned into a story told over and over again. The hike to Forest Lake has become part of our family lore as Helane continues to ask me to "tell about our hike" again and again. Piper was twelve days old when we first took her hiking. Our objective was Hermann Lake, about three miles from the trailhead and 2,000 feet up. The Hermann Gulch Trail is popular for ski touring, and we had skied a mile or so with Helane during the winter before Piper was born. The weather was lovely for a hike, and I was particularly anxious to get into the mountains. To carry Piper, I used a Gerry front carrier which I covered with a flannel receiving blanket and a crocheted blanket to protect her from the breeze and sun. The blankets were secured underneath the carrier's shoulder straps and tucked up underneath. The weight held the blankets in place. As always seems to be the case with the Gerry front carrier, I could not walk with both arms swinging freely but had to constantly support Piper's head with one hand. However, that seemed preferable to carrying her in the Snugli in which she would have been completely buried simply because of the relative sizes of baby and carrier. On my back I carried our daypack with water, lunch, and sweaters. Dean carried the aluminum-framed Gerry carrier for Helane to ride in when she tired.

As we left the car, Helane, Dean, and I were a curious trio. Helane was carrying her small daypack containing her sweatshirt and a plastic thermos of lemonade; I carried the bundled item on my front and a daypack on my back; and Dean carried an empty child carrier. Within a half mile, however, Helane hopped aboard. Now three years and eight months old, she weighed thirty-seven pounds—this made it the last season she would be carried.

We worked our way up the trail singing songs and telling stories. Helane walked and rode to suit her fancy. To me the most delightful times were when I was walking behind Dean and Helane listening to her singing an endless, improvised song.

We stopped to take photographs and drink water and eat snacks at intervals so frequent that I wondered whether or not we would ever reach the lake. When it became clear that she had no further intention of walking *up* the trail, Dean shouldered his heavy load and informed me they would meet

"Mmmmnnn. Peanut butter and jelly. Our favorite!" Medicine Bow Peak, Wyoming. *Jung Family Photo.*

me at the lake.

I proceeded at a slow but steady pace along with Piper, who slept peacefully the entire time. When I finally arrived at the lake, Dean and Helane were almost ready to leave. The lake was still almost completely frozen with just the slightest thawing around the edge. The cliffs surrounding the lake formed a magnificent cirque. I felt pleased at having accomplished our objective. I also felt I had to rest and eat my sandwich. Predictably, as soon as I stopped walking and sat down, Piper started to scream. I tried to nurse her, but she wasn't interested. She didn't want a bottle either. I quickly put a long-legged, long-sleeved sleeper with feet on her in case she was cold. Her screams bounced and echoed around the cirque. There were several other hikers there whom I knew had hiked this far to enjoy the peace and quiet that existed at the lake before Piper and I arrived. I gulped down a sandwich and started down the trail. Eventually, the move-

"Gees, that water's moving pretty fast down there." Idaho's Sawtooths. *Martin Family Photo.*

ment lulled Piper into sleep once again. When she was quiet I slowed my pace to a near standstill (stopping might have provoked another outburst) until Dean and Helane caught up with me.

Since Piper was warm, in clean diapers, and presented with food at the lake—all the things that normally made her happy—I'm inclined to blame her screaming on the altitude. I don't know whether or not she had a headache or some other altitude-related discomfort, but when we descended the trail for some distance, she calmed down. Since young children can't explain exactly how they feel bad, parents should keep in mind that the altitude may affect youngsters just as it does adults, even though, if they're being carried,

"Who's that tough guy behind those Foster Grants?" Protect those eyes from day one. *Jung Family Photo.*

the children are not exerting themselves.

We could see storm clouds coming up the valley and determined to beat the rain if we could. Helane found walking downhill much more to her liking and walked with us at a reasonable pace to numerous choruses of "Little Red Caboose Chug, Chug, Chug" in which we all took repeated turns at being the engine or the caboose. When it became clear that we were not going to escape the rain, Helane got into the Gerry carrier for a last mad dash before the clouds opened. As the rain started, Dean put on a poncho which adequately protected him and Helane. I wore a pullover waterproof parka large enough to fit over Piper, and it kept us both dry. I kept checking to see that Piper could breathe, buried as she was under blankets and inside the parka. She appeared blissfully cozy. In the semi-darkness underneath Dean's poncho, Helane fell asleep. We tried a sweater as a make-shift pillow that would provide some stability for her head, but it was nearly impossible to keep her weight from shifting from one side to the other. She was a hard load to carry.

As is so often the case, the storm was intense but brief, and before we reached the car the rain had given way to a rainbow. Helane woke up when we took off the poncho and walked the final quarter mile to the car. Other than for Dean's sore shoulders, the hike was a definite success.

CHICAGO LAKES:
Equipment Only Breaks When You Need It

Having experienced a successful first hike, we were anxious to go hiking again en famille and asked friends to join us the next weekend for a hike to Chicago Lakes near Mount Evans. We started hiking at Echo Lake on the trail which descends steeply into the Chicago Creek drainage. Starting a hike by going down is rather novel and appealed to Helane a great deal. There were a few stretches of trail, however, that had enough exposure—steep dropoffs—that Dean opted to carry her. Our friends James and Felicity brought their daughter Genevieve, eighteen months old. Genevieve rode in a Gerry carrier on her father's back. I carried Piper and daypack, Dean carried Helane when necessary, and Felicity carried their daypack. Helane informed us she would not carry a pack. As long as she carried herself a little more than she had last week, that was acceptable. Just past the Idaho Springs reservoir, we took a long break. Helane consumed her lunch. The rest of us deferred in anticipation of lunching at the first lake.

The next stretch of the trail was particularly lovely. Once past a couple of switchbacks, it leveled out and passed through an area that once burned in a forest fire. Though the wildflowers were not yet in full bloom, lush greenery abounded. Helane was able to walk from this point to the spot where we stopped for lunch—a quarter mile or so from the first lake. As the weather appeared to be deteriorating, and we had a fine view of the lake and waterfall, we found a nice spot to picnic among some rocks next to the trail. Piper had once again slept for

Kids and water *definitely* attract. *Martin Family Photo.*

the duration of the hike, but now she woke up, as hungry for lunch as the rest of us.

As we finished eating, the wind increased and we packed up for our return trip. The hike down the trail was quite pleasant. Helane happily walked large portions of it, and when she rode, she and Genevieve talked to each other. At the reservoir we took a break and ate a snack. When we reassembled everything to leave, Helane wanted to ride. But as soon as we put her in the Gerry carrier, she started screaming that her legs hurt. Closer inspection revealed the cause. The aluminum frame of the carrier had collapsed, and Helane's legs were being smashed. After she was extricated, we tried to bend the carrier back into its original form, but the aluminum frame broke. The carrier was useless. Helane easily walked the next portion of the trail (which is actually an access road to the reservoir), but at the point where we had to leave the road and hike up the trail which we had descended at the outset, we faced a minor crisis: Helane insisted she couldn't walk any further. James kindly volunteered their Gerry carrier and said he would carry Genevieve in his arms or on his shoulders. Helane immediately fell asleep in the carrier. Genevieve, however, decided that she preferred walking and proceeded most of the way back to the car, protesting loudly whenever James picked her up and carried her over the rocky places.

If there's a moral to the story of this hike, it's this: Don't become too dependent on any piece of equipment. If you do, it will surely break.

UNNAMED LAKE:
Another Kind of First Step

On July 4 we drove to Aspen, Colorado. When we arrived, we located the house we had rented for the long weekend, then decided to go for a hike before dinner and fireworks. We set out for an unnamed lake recommended by the home-owner. After hiking a very reasonable three-quarters of a mile along a road, we found the lake and went down to cool our feet. Apparently, there was a spring at the edge of the lake, and Helane mushed her feet about in the mud. We watched a herd of cows grazing near the end of the lake, ducks skimming across the water, and a mother duck taking her ducklings for a swim. Then the mosquitoes found us, and we quickly moved on. Dean suggested finding a different way back to our house, and Helane and I enthusiastically agreed. Three-week-old Piper was sleeping as usual and made no comment. The way back, of course, was longer than we expected. Biting flies turned their attention from the cows to us and pursued us relentlessly and made us very uncomfortable. We rushed through a giant aspen grove and hiked up a steep incline to find ourselves on a ridge, well above and quite a ways from our house.

This high ground provided a splendid ridge-walk for close to half a mile. It was Helane's first opportunity to hike in such an exposed location, and we all enjoyed the excellent views. Even a short hike had become an adventure because of the dramatic ridge. Experiencing the ridge-walk was a first for all of us—a true discovery for Helane and a delightful rediscovery of the wonder of it for Dean and me.

A family hike does not have to be long or require advance planning to provide an opportunity for wonderful discovery. The most important thing is taking the first step out the door.

AMERICAN LAKE:
Sticking To the Plan—And Together

The next day we arranged with Lizzie and Bailey, a couple of friends from Boston who were visiting Aspen, to join us on a hike to American Lake, three miles and a couple of thousand vertical feet from the trailhead. The lake is located not far from Cathedral Lake, but is apparently a much less popular hike. On this occasion Lizzie, Bailey, Piper, and I started out together. Dean and Helane planned to meet us at the lake following a morning of golf. Within a half-mile Bailey decided the pace was too slow and he took off on his own, planning to meet us at the lake at the same time Dean was to be there.

Lizzie and I set a leisurely pace which allowed us to visit with each other. There was no time pressure, and when Piper woke up and began to fuss, we stopped in a lush meadow while I fed her. With Piper fed and freshly diapered, we continued our hike and arrived at American Lake a half hour before the appointed rendezvous time. Right on schedule, Dean arrived carrying Helane asleep on his back in our new Gerry carrier. He had carried her almost the entire way. We ate lunch on an outcropping of land which is almost an island in the lake, and looked in vain for Bailey. We thought we saw someone in the talus far above and beyond, then eventually decided it was either a tall rock or a short tree. At the final time deadline we had set, Lizzie, Dean, Helane, Piper, and I

"Boy, but they do get heavy fast." *Jung Family Photo.*

started down the trail wondering where Bailey might be. At
the beautiful meadow we stopped for another baby feeding
and general admiration of the spot. As we were gathering
ourselves to leave, Bailey arrived, humming cheerfully to himself. Our party complete, we hiked out together. Helane hiked
all the way down from American Lake, three miles, her longest
hike to date.

Even though we met up with Bailey without any ado, it should be noted that this was not good form. Everyone should follow basic safety procedures, whether hiking with or without children. It is always something of a risk for a member of any party to hike alone. Had we not encountered our friend again, we would have arrived at the trailhead with two tired, cranky kids who needed to be taken home, only to be faced with the logistical problem of driving back to the trailhead later to find Bailey.

Even small risks may need to be evaluated differently when hiking with children. Sitting around at the trailhead for a few hours waiting for a possibly lost member of the party is no big thing for a group of adults. But it's a much less attractive prospect with a couple of kids. When hiking with children, minimize risk. Don't take chances!

"We always give nature the right-of-way." Glacier National Park. *Jung Family Photo.*

"A fella's got to keep his head on straight out here in the wilderness."
Borneman Family Photo.

"Sure doesn't *taste* like tomato juice." *Borneman Family Photo.*

"He's quiet now, but if Dad doesn't start moving soon, there's gonna be BIG trouble." *Borneman Family Photo.*

CRATER LAKE:
An Adult Disaster

July 6 was a day for the fast hikers to extend themselves and for Helane to set her own distance record. Lizzie and Bailey, our friends from Boston; Jack and Mary, friends from Boulder, Colorado; Ann and her dog Rosie from Denver; Dean, Helane, Piper, and I took the bus from the Highlands parking lot to Maroon Lake. We split up almost immediately. The serious hikers headed for Buckskin Pass, while Helane, Piper, and I headed for Crater Lake two miles from the trailhead. This was a major experiment. As usual, I carried Piper in a front carrier and a daypack on my back, but Helane was on her own—we had no Gerry carrier for her to get into when she got tired. She would walk the entire way—or the entire way would be determined by how far she would walk. The entire way turned out to be the full two miles to Crater Lake. She took it at a leisurely pace, accompanied by songs and storytelling, and broken by numerous snack and water stops. The trail was very open as we neared the lake, and the day was hot. We found ourselves hiking from one spot of shade to the next. We passed a family hiking with a three-month-old baby and carrying camping equipment for an overnight. Mother had the baby in a front Snugli and an ill-fitting, overloaded daypack on her back; Dad carried a large, apparently heavy Kelty frame pack with the majority of the equipment. The way was not going smoothly for them. Mother's load appeared much too unwieldy. We last saw them just before we all reached Crater Lake. They were planning to go a couple of miles beyond the lake, but whether or not they reached their destination, they had already reached a number of lovely campsites at the lake and a beautiful setting for their overnight.

At the lake, Helane, Piper, and I stopped for lunch, and by chance we met our friend Mary, who had decided not to hike all the way to the pass. We ate in the shade of a huge spruce tree and waded in the lake. Helane discovered an extremely entertaining water toy—a heavy, clear, plastic bag which she filled and refilled with lake water. As a bonus, it contained tiny polywogs each time we inspected its contents!

"Com'on Mom, let's get going!" *Jung Family Photo.*

The journey back to the traihead was easier than the uphill hike to the lake. It required fewer stops, but more uninterrupted story telling.

Perhaps it's a comment on my lack of imagination or the folklore of the times, but the stories I've found most useful for hiking are stories about movies Helane has seen. Thus, the trail from Maroon Lake to Crater Lake is now indelibly associated in my mind, and perhaps in Helane's, with "The Karate Kid."

When we reached Maroon Lake, we waited for the bus and the rest of our party. The bus we had agreed to catch came and went. I grew impatient. Then a couple of other hikers asked me if I was waiting for a tall man with a mustache and glasses. When I replied yes, they told me that it would be a while before he arrived. He had fallen while running down the trail and apparently broken something.

Half an hour later, a gray-faced Dean appeared, supported by Jack on one side and Lizzie on the other. He was in severe pain. No doubt he'd broken something! Once we got him to Aspen Valley Hospital, the emergency room doctor confirmed the trailhead diagnosis: Dean's right hip socket had a long fracture in it.

A worst-case hypothetical situation had unfortunately come true: On a hike with kids, an adult had broken a bone and had to be carried out. In this case we had not been depending on Dean to carry either of the children; the hike had been planned so Helane could go on her own; we were on a well-traveled trail—not a remote wilderness area; and we had other adults who gave Dean the assistance he needed to get to the trailhead. Despite such a serious accident, it did not require much imagination for us to realize how lucky we had been.

Many families make it a practice to include an extra adult or two on their outings. It makes excellent sense. Having experienced the value of having extra adults along, we now always try to do so.

OBSERVATIONS:
And Some Helpful Hints

(1) Choose an attractive objective for the hike.

(2) If your child is of marginal hiking age, take along a carrier so that you can carry him or her if necessary.

(3) Take adequate rain gear. It can make the difference between a pleasant hike on a damp day and a cold, wet, miserable experience.

(4) Always carry extra hats, mittens, and jackets in case the weather changes.

(5) Use sun hats, sunglasses, and sunblock to protect your children's sensitive skin and eyes.

(6) Take lots of snack and lunch breaks. They are especially important to keep children's bodies well fueled and their blood sugar level from dropping too low.

(7) Take along some extra treats to use as encouragement to hike up the next-to-last hill.

(8) Don't be overambitious—plan a route that allows time for examining flowers and splashing in streams.

(9) And always remember: Safety first.

"This hat happens to be one of my favorites, pardner." *White Family Photo.*

Chapter Four

Horsepacking

Betsy White's motto is "Use whatever help you can get: whenever from whomever." Her motto is appropriately applied to friends—and also to pack animals. They're especially appealing after you've carried a double load while your spouse carried a child.

A dozen years ago, Betsy and her family and eighteen other friends horsepacked into the Wind River Mountains of Wyoming for five days. The group consisted of married couples and their children, several father-son and father-daughter teams (the children ranging from three to eleven years old), and a few college students. It was the Fourth of July. The party started out from Big Sandy Lodge headed for the Cirque of the Towers. The wranglers in front led the pack animals, the men traveled on foot, and the women and children followed on saddle horses. Betsy's youngest child Laura was only one year old, and Betsy carried her in a front pack.

It was a dozen miles to the first campsite, which was located at the base of Jackass Pass, but at ten miles the party reached the snow line. The trail was slippery with mud, the horses were skittery, and the wranglers determined that it was unsafe to continue. The horses were unpacked and the loads shifted to the human packers. The wranglers returned to the lodge with the horses and agreed to meet the campers at the snow line four days hence.

The last two miles to the campsite were rough going. Betsy carried a full Kelty pack on her back and Laura on the front. Six-year-old Eric walked, but three-year-old Greg required some assistance from his dad, Gene, who also carried the rest of the camping and climbing gear.

After a night at the base of Jackass Pass, the party split up into two groups. One headed for the unparalleled rock climbing opportunities in the Cirque of the Towers; the other group headed for the fishing opportunities provided by Big Sandy Lake. High winds discouraged fishing on the second day of the trip, however, and on the third day the campers woke up to find themselves encompassed by a mantle of fresh fallen snow. But by afternoon the snow had melted, and day four dawned magnificent. That day fishermen and climbers alike enjoyed great success in their respective endeavors. On day five everyone reluctantly hiked back to the main trail and met the horses.

Jane Bunin, her husband Mike Yokell, and their two sons, Ben and Abe, have twice ventured into the Wind River Mountains of Wyoming with the assistance of horses. On both trips they began at Dickinson Park on the east side of the Wind Rivers near the Popo Agie Wilderness Area. The outfitters' camp is just north of the Cirque of the Towers, and from there they enjoyed wonderful views of those spectacular peaks. Both Jane and Mike are very goal-oriented, and that is as true in their recreation as in their work. The routes they chose for their Wind River trips involved a twelve- to fifteen-mile horseback ride on the first day, followed by five days of hiking a circuitous route over passes and through valleys which brought them back to the outfitters' camp. The long ride on the first day of their trip allowed them to penetrate deeply into the wilderness with a full load of food. They were also able to accomplish the first elevation gain with a minimum of difficulty. On both trips they have been accompanied by additional adults. Because riding a full day on a horse can be uncomfortable to anyone not used to it, Jane and Mike arranged for fewer than one horse per person. One pack horse

"And we're off!" *Martin Family Photo.*

carried their family's camping gear and backpacks. Another pack horse carried their friends' gear. Members of the party rode two saddle horses in shifts. The outfitters were happy to arrange a "drop trip" of this sort. By planning a route that allowed them to hike back to the outfitters' camp, the Bunin/ Yokell family obtained maximum efficiency from the horses for a minimum cost.

During their first trip to the Wind Rivers, the weather was very wet—it rained day after day. The family remained in good spirits, Jane believes, because both she and Mike were so comfortable living outdoors that the bad weather didn't particularly bother them. Because their parents were relaxed and able to enjoy their vacation despite the rain, the boys were also.

On their second trip to the Wind Rivers, their route was more ambitious than that of their first trip—they planned to hike between six and eight miles on each of the five hiking

"Maybe later, he'll let me hold the reins." *White Family Photo.*

days. The horses dropped them off at 9,000 feet and their circle backpack took them over two 11,000-foot passes. The weather was good, but, to be safe, they arose very early on each of the pass-crossing days and hiked over the passes before any electrical activity could develop in connection with an afternoon thunderstorm.

Jane and Mike believe that any trip they plan should be well within their children's capabilities. They plan routes and hiking distances to allow time for examining rocks and flowers and playing in streams. They are also willing to challenge their children, however, and they know that Abe may require the promise of a piece of chocolate at the top of the pass to encourage him to do his best. All the trips they plan are also well within their own capabilities, so that in the event of an emergency, they know they will have sufficient personal reserves to respond.

Horsepacking trips need not last so long. One family we know which has had successful experiences horsepacking with their children is in the fortunate position of not having to hire horses—they own their own. Bob and Maggie Taylor had Marissa and Sam on horseback before the children could walk. At first Maggie carried the baby in a front pack. Then the baby graduated to a backpack. Eventually, she rode on the saddle in front of Maggie. Now four-year-old Marissa rides her own horse solo and Sam is riding in front of Maggie.

One successful overnight horse trip was taken from their ranch house to a sheepherder's wagon located in a far corner of their property. After about a two-hour ride through the pine forest, the trees disappeared and the country opened up into sagebrush plains. Two hours seems to be about the maximum ride for a child who is sitting on the saddle. A younger child riding in a front or back pack can ride longer— that's determined by the parents' stamina!

The family entourage sighted the lonely sheepherder's wagon some distance away standing next to a single tree in a small clearing. As they approached, they seemed to have been transported into another time when all travel was on horseback. The sheepherder himself might have been just over the hill watching his flock. The family enjoyed a quiet campfire under the stars by themselves. Maggie and the children turned into their beds inside the wagon—modern-day gypsies— while Bob slept outside to listen to the coyotes sing. They spent the morning leisurely exploring the nearby area on foot, then Bob and Maggie loaded up the horses, and the family spent the afternoon riding back into the twentieth century.

The Taylors' overnight to the sheepherder's wagon was uneventful—perhaps the highest compliment that can be given to a camping trip involving both children and horses. The destination of the sheepherder's wagon provided a clear objective for the outing. Spending the night in the wagon was exotic—an historic and cultural experience, a perfect example of experiential education.

It is certainly appealing to be able to ride a horse into a campsite leading a pack horse carrying the gear; however, even if you walk, it greatly lessens the load to have a pack animal carry the gear.

Burros are famous (and infamous) pack animals. In California, there are a number of pack stations which will provide them for pack trips. Alice Alldredge and her husband Jim King took their son Matthew on such a trip when he was seventeen months old. They rented a burro and hired a guide who packed them in to a base camp in Mineral King in Sequoia National Park, where they camped for a week. From there they took numerous day hikes, sometimes all together, sometimes alternating child care responsibilities. On the appointed day the packer and burro returned to pack them out to civilization. They found the system efficient and effective. They were able to establish their base camp further from the trailhead than would have been possible had they carried all their gear plus Matthew, and they traveled in a much more comfortable fashion.

In Colorado, California, and elsewhere, it's possible to hire llamas to carry equipment just as the burros do. Llamas, which have carried loads throughout the Andes since Inca times, are remarkably well suited to the task. If overloaded, they are known to sit down and spit, but otherwise they are gentle creatures.

My first experience horsepacking with children was a comedy of errors. When Helane was two years old, we arranged with a horsepacker near Durango in the San Juan Mountains of Colorado to take Dean, Helane, myself, and one other couple and their thirteen-year-old daughter on a week-long trip. We were hoping to see some new country and do some peak climbing. We worked hard with the guide to determine a route that would satisfy everyone. Unfortunately, the weather was against us. Just before the trip began, it rained all day every day. The rain fell in such quantities that the guide who had lived there for sixty years couldn't remember anything like it. Hay was rotting in the fields. It was too wet to bale and there was no sun to dry it. The mountain trails were so deep in mud that the horses sank to their knees.

In increasingly discouraging telephone conversations, the guide told us of how the horses had slipped and lunged over the rocks on the steep trails on his previous week's trip. Then he told me that despite the rain, his grandson had been exercising a pony for Helane to ride. I didn't understand. I had thought Helane would be riding on the saddle in front of me. Then it was his turn to be confused. He had understood Helane was seven years old—too big to be sharing a saddle. Then I felt bad. Helane was two years old, not seven—too small *not* to share a saddle. When we finished untangling matters, the guide declared he didn't consider it safe to take such a small child where we were planning to go in light of the miserable conditions. We were in Denver, three hundred miles away, and when the guide said it wasn't safe because of the weather conditions, we were in no position to argue with him.

I did present some alternatives, such as: (1) if it's not safe for me to ride with her, maybe you could take her on your saddle and I'll lead the pack horses; and (2) if it's too muddy for anyone to ride with Helane, I'll walk and carry her in a back pack. Neither suggestion received a positive response. The guide neither wanted to take on the responsibility of riding with a client's child under difficult conditions nor wanted to allow a client to lead his pack string. His objection to the alternative of hiking and carrying Helane was that the horses moved much faster than a hiker; the party would get split up; distances were so far that the hiker wouldn't make it to the campsite; to him the idea in principle was completely impractical.

The guide was probably as disappointed to lose our business as we were to cancel our trip, but given the weather and the misunderstanding about Helane's age, it seemed the best thing to do. The guide graciously refunded our deposit, and we learned one more lesson in the importance of clear communication.

That experience has not completely discouraged us. We still do hope to take a horsepacking trip in some upcoming season.

The expense of a horsepack trip should be noted. The cost per animal is at least twenty-five dollars per day. If the animals can be used to deliver gear to a campsite and then return some days later, the cost may not be overwhelming. If you plan to move from spot to spot, however, and the horses will be required to move you, the cost increases dramatically. Even if the horses are taking a rest day between moves, you will have to pay for them as well as for the guide.

Burros are somewhat cheaper; llamas, however, are not. If economy is the most important factor, for better or worse, we'll be loading our own packs to double-weight and staggering on.

If you use pack animals for a day to carry gear to a base camp, there is no requirement for specialized equipment. If you are planning a multi-day horsepacking trip, however, there will be some significant differences. They are not so much a matter of equipment as a matter of style. Of course, you'll need some footgear with heels so your feet don't slip through the stirrups; cowboy boots, designed for that purpose, are the best thing to wear. Any long pants will keep the saddle from chafing your legs, but a pair of Levis would be the traditional choice. Freeze-dried food is not required because the horses are able to carry the extra weight of fresh eggs and bacon, steak, and potatoes. All in all, a horsepack trip can be much more luxurious than a backpacking trip can possibly be.

A meeting of cultures on the trail in Nepal. *White Family Photo.*

Horsepacking is certainly not limited to the United States. In fact, it is much more acceptable in many other countries because it is still a commonly used mode of transportation.

Betsy White's first experiences with horsepacking with children was in Pakistan in 1966. Her son Eric was born in Pakistan, where she and her husband Gene were living following a two-year tour in the Peace Corps. Gene, a water engineer, had worked for the Pakistani government for three years. During that time the Whites made several expeditions into the Karakorams. In Pakistan the glaciated valleys leading into the mountains are many miles long. Local custom dictates that people who can afford to, mountaineers included, ride these distances on horseback rather than trek through them

Horsepacking in the Kaghan Valley, Pakistan, 1967.
White Family Photo.

on foot. When Eric was three, the Whites rode horses into a beautiful, remote valley. One guide led the pack string and a second guide led Eric's horse. From their base camp, Gene and Betsy took turns watching Eric and climbing the 20,000-foot peaks that surrounded them. After a week had passed, the guides returned with the horses, and they packed out again.

In Nepal, the trails are too steep and treacherous for pack animals. There, the time-honored tradition is to pay porters to carry your load. Some, however, will carry loads only as far as the snow line, but others, the Sherpas, famous for their mountaineering skills, have climbed as high as the summit of Mount Everest. In 1977, Betsy White and her family were in Nepal determined to trek to the Annapurna Sanctuary. Eric was thirteen years old; Greg nine; and Laura seven. The objective of the trip was not a climb, but the journey itself. The Nepalese porters are accustomed to carrying loads considered extraordinary by western standards. At seven years old, Laura was well within the weight limit which a porter was willing to carry. Betsy arranged for Laura to have her own porter to carry her whenever she got too tired to walk, though Laura, a strong young hiker, never availed herself of the opportunity to ride on her porter's back. They spent approximately three weeks on their journey, one week en route to the sanctuary, one week camping there, and one week returning. Few of us may ever enjoy the opportunity to trek in Nepal, but what an incomparable experience it was for the Whites and their children!

OBSERVATIONS:
And Some Helpful Hints

Horsepacking may enable your family to travel distances and visit places that are too difficult to reach by backpacking alone.

(1) Different kinds of horsepack trips are available, ranging from completely catered trips, riding horses every day, accompanied by a guide and wranglers, to a bare bones drop trip.

(2) On drop trips, not everyone needs a saddle horse. Pack horses can carry equipment and people can alternate hiking and riding.

(3) Burros and llamas are also available for pack trips or drop trips.

(4) Think creatively about how to use pack animals to achieve the best possible wilderness experience for your family.

"Ah, this is the life!" *Neely Family Photo.*

Chapter Five

Canoeing

W ater sports such as rafting, kayaking, and canoeing present special hazards to youngsters. Since children are not very powerful, even if they are able to swim, once overboard they are at the mercy of the water until an adult can pull them out. There are special lifejackets available that have collars on them and which are constructed so that a child will float on his or her back, head out of the water. The water is unforgiving, however, and two or three minutes underwater can result in effects much more devastating than almost anything that can happen on land. Because of that, water sports are less appropriate than most land sports for very young children.

Between canoeing, rafting, and kayaking, canoeing is the safest and most enjoyable for children. Rafting done on rivers where the current is strong is hazardous because if a child falls overboard, he or she will be swept away by the current. Kayaking is inappropriate because of the restrictive nature of the cockpit and sprayskirt. But canoeing allows a child some freedom of movement and can be done on bodies of water which are not moving rapidly. This makes a spill over the side less dangerous.

Once a child is five years old or older, canoeing has advantages that may outweigh the disadvantages. First, the distance to be traveled need not be limited by how far a child can walk. For example, canoeing in the Boundary Waters in northern Minnesota, our friend Mike Yokell found that he could paddle for hours; he traveled many miles with little difficulty, far more than his five-year-old son Benjamin could have walked. Second, the canoe could take more equipment more comfortably than Mike could have carried on his back. Third, by choosing a route with only a few short portages, Mike minimized the number of times he had to carry the gear. It was important that Mike was strong enough to carry the canoe by himself because young Ben was not able to provide much assistance. On the portages they did do, Mike made one trip carrying the canoe, then retraced his steps and made a second trip carrying the equipment. Because he didn't feel he could safely leave Ben at either end of the portage, Ben walked back and forth with Mike carrying small loads of gear.

My friend Cindy Neely began canoeing with her son Burr when he was five years old. Their first trip was a peaceful stretch of river in New Hampshire. Burr had been car camping on numerous occasions, but this was his first wilderness trip. The party consisted of two canoes, Cindy's friend Christine, and Cindy's son Ted, twelve years older than Burr. There were no thrilling rapids to be found on the river Cindy chose, and she was not seeking that kind of excitement and danger. Instead, Cindy and her party were on the river to unwind, to slow down. The enjoyment they sought was in the solitude of the forest-lined river and the beauty of the sunset. For five days they got away from ordinary routine, floated downstream, and camped on the river banks at night. Burr discovered an entirely new rhythm of life.

It is this peace, this rhythm, that Cindy has sought and found over and over again in her thirty-five years of canoeing. She, too, began canoeing as a child in the eastern United States. When her older son Ted was eleven years old, he begged to be allowed to go on a canoe trip. Those trips were so successful that Cindy felt confident about introducing her younger son Burr to the sport at an even younger age.

The summer after Burr's first expedition, he was invited to

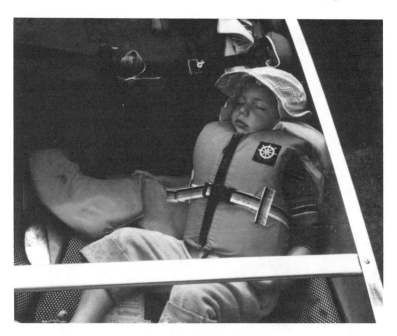

"It's the rocking . . . sort of makes me . . . sleepy . . . ."
Bunin Family Photo.

go on a canoe trip with his two seven-year-old cousins. Burr's aunt, uncle, brother Ted, and Ted's friend paddled a stretch of the Allegash River in Maine. Although Ted and his friend, both eighteen at the time, were adults in terms of strength and canoeing ability, they were youthful enough that Burr's aunt and uncle found the child-to-adult ratio inadequate and therefore mentally exhausting. Experience indicates that there should be at least one adult for every child under ten, and two adults per child if possible. Though it may have been exhausting for the adults involved, Burr returned full of enthusiasm for his next canoeing adventure.

In some ways, canoeing on a river is easier than canoeing on a lake. Even though the stretch of river may be flat, there is always some current to carry the canoe downstream. Unless the river is very wide, wind is not a severe problem and the force of the current will almost always keep the boat moving forward. If there are any portages involved on a river trip,

"Are you sure it goes that way, Mom?" *Neely Family Photo.*

they will be done to avoid some hazard, such as a rapid or a waterfall. If the trip is well planned, such portages will be short, and in many cases, if the hazard is a rapid, the adults may be able to run the canoes through while the children walk around; so the canoes may not have to be carried at all.

One obvious advantage of canoeing with children is the opportunity to travel many miles, independent of a child's ability to hike, but even so, numbers and strength are still important. One adult and one child may be able to handle a canoe, depending on how strong the adult is. Any party, how-ever, is much better off and better able to deal with any emergencies if there are two adults and one child per canoe. Portages also require strength to carry canoes and gear; thus, a weaker party may enjoy a quiet river trip more than a trip on a number of lakes.

Taking a break in the Boundary Waters. *Neely Family Photo.*

Burr's third season of canoeing included a trip which Cindy had dreamed of for years—a trip to the Boundary Waters of Minnesota. Along with the contiguous Quetico Wilderness Area of Canada, they cover hundreds of square miles.

The trip to the Boundary Waters was Cindy's first experience canoeing on a lake with Burr, and from it she learned a great deal. As usual, the party consisted of two canoes to carry three adults plus Burr. Although some people plan circle trips through the Boundary Waters, Cindy intended to camp on the fifth lake into the wilderness the first night and establish a base camp there. The fifth lake meant just that—there were four portages to be accomplished before arriving at the fifth lake. And that proved difficult for three adults and one child. The group didn't have enough strength to do this comfortably, and Cindy later decided not to do that many portages again

"We outdoor types got to be prepared for all kinds of weather."
Neely Family Photo.

without more adults in the party.

Once they reached lake five and established their base camp, however, the trip turned out to be everything they had hoped. On each of the three successive days they took canoe trips. Since they carried only a daypack with a lunch, portages meant only a single trip carrying the canoe. They ranged far and wide on these excursions, but each night returned to their familiar, if temporary, home. Burr especially enjoyed fishing in his "home waters" at sunset, and the rest of the party enjoyed his success.

Another trip that became a favorite of Cindy and Burr was the Missouri River in Montana. The river is slow and wide and a heavy wind may almost blow a canoe upstream, but the scenery is unparalleled and the fishing good.

One drizzly morning, Burr was in the bow of the canoe fishing. Cindy's friend Christine was asleep in the middle, and Cindy was in the stern gently guiding the canoe. Burr appeared to be half asleep. Suddenly his line went taut, the whole canoe felt the jolt, and Burr instinctively dropped to his knees to begin reeling in the fish. Then he gave a final pull on his rod to bring in the catch. As he pulled up and turned around, the flopping fish hit Christine in the head. She bolted upright and flung out her arms in self-defense. The canoe rocked precariously for a few seconds. Cindy struggled to control the canoe as it turned around and around in the middle of the river. Finally, the canoe settled back to an even keel. It was an exciting catch and an excellent dinner! But the memory pointed out the need to be always alert on the water!

Later, on that same trip, as the party drifted slowly downstream, it was overtaken by a boatload of Montana fish and game wardens. They had been doing some fishing themselves and presented Burr with a string of whitefish. On the fifth day of the trip, from the depths of the food duffel, Cindy produced a fresh lemon. That night, the party feasted on whitefish poached in white wine with fresh lemon and butter sauce.

Based on her experience, Cindy has some equipment suggestions:

(1) Packing gear. Pack everything in duffel bags lined with plastic garbage bags. Make extensive lists of what each person will take and what each duffel will hold. Cindy also packs the duffels keeping in mind the person who will carry them when portaging. Food is put in daypacks. In the top of one daypack is the "snack kit," which consists of a sterno stove, sierra cups, a pot, and packages of instant soup and tea. On a rainy day

Ready to shove off. *Neely Family Photo.*

quick access to the snack foods and the ability to prepare a quick cup of something hot to drink are essential to the well-being of the party. The snack kit is the last item put into the canoe because it will be the first and possibly only item unpacked at the morning break.

Cindy also includes one night of shakedown camping at the beginning of the trip, usually en route to the put in. The objective is to make sure that everything fits into its pack or duffel as it should, and that once unpacked, the duffels can be repacked in the morning.

(2) Essential items include rain jackets with sleeves that close tightly at the wrists. If the sleeves don't close, every time you paddle, water runs down the sleeve to the elbow. The jacket should either have a hood or fasten tightly around

the neck. A sou'wester hat with its front bill is also considered essential equipment. It keeps the rain out of your eyes and off your neck. A second type—a mosquito hat—is also standard equipment. It has a broad brim with mosquito netting that can be pulled down to protect the face and neck when necessary. It is also imperative to carry bug repellent, although it won't substitute for a mosquito hat. Also include a long-sleeved shirt and long pants for protection against insects as much as protection against the sun or the cold, although shorts, t-shirts, and swimming suits are the preferred attire whenever weather and insect life permit.

(3) Wear lifejackets whenever you're on the water. It's hard to convince a child to wear one if the adults don't wear theirs. Conversely, if the adults put their lifejackets on, children automatically imitate them by putting theirs on, too. Unless they are accomplished swimmers, children should have lifejackets that are designed to turn them right side up and keep their heads out of the water.

(4) For traveling by canoe, everyone should wear boat shoes. These are not flip-flops or other footgear that can be easily kicked off. Ideally they are old tennis shoes with holes which allow water and air to flow through their sides. There is a great temptation for children to go barefoot in a canoe, but that's hazardous. When the party stops to have a snack or camp, a child in the bow is often the first one to jump out of the canoe with the bowline. It's too late to scramble to put shoes on at that point and, jumping out, it's easy to land on sharp rocks, pointed sticks, or even broken glass. Once again, an example set by adults seems the easiest way to keep boat shoes on children's feet.

(5) Cindy and her family carry two tie-on items that don't go in duffels—a two-burner Coleman stove and Chiquita, a ten-dollar camping guitar, each protected by cases and plastic bags. Items like that distinguish canoeing from backpacking. Too heavy and awkward to carry, they make a great difference in the convenience and ambience of a camp. A friend of mine

"Better watch out, John Denver." *Neely Family Photo.*

who kayaks doesn't have room for a guitar, but because he recognizes the importance of music around the campfire, he carries what he calls the Band—a kazoo, finger cymbals, spoons, drumsticks, and a harmonica. They fit into a small stuff sack. Music around the campfire is a source of wonderful memories, important for children and adults alike.

(6) For additional personal gear, include long underwear, socks, jackets, wool hats, gloves, and a second pair of footgear. Dry shoes are essential for wearing around camp at the end of the day. The only way to keep the second pair dry is to finish all the chores before putting them on. Pull up the canoes, flip them over, and set up camp first. Too many times that one last water-related chore has meant two wet pair of shoes at the end of the day. Ugh!

One skill that should not be overlooked in canoeing is the importance of orienteering—the ability to use a map and compass. The portage from one lake to another may be well concealed along the overgrown shoreline and easily missed if you misread the map. Also, keep maps and compass in truly watertight containers. A soggy map tears easily and is no fun to read!

Considering her many years of canoeing, it's interesting that Cindy Neely does not own her own canoe. She prefers to rent. The cost of renting a canoe, lifejackets, and paddles is nominal—about ten dollars per day. Balanced against the expense of owning, maintaining, and transporting a canoe to the put in—for Cindy usually at least a day's drive—it makes better sense. The only equipment she suggests purchasing is a child's paddle. Her experience has shown that canoe outfitters usually don't have children's paddles. It is terribly frustrating for a child to be unable to paddle—an adult's paddle is too large for a child to handle.

Jane Bunin, who has been on several canoe trips with her husband Mike Yokell and their two sons, Ben and Abe, purchased the boys' first paddles from an Indian craftsman who sold his wares at an old fort along the shore of Lake Superior. Since then, they have replaced those paddles with slightly larger ones they bought at a hardware store for less than ten dollars apiece. Jane also recommends purchasing your own child-sized lifejackets. She considers rentals unsafe—you can't be sure of them. In fact, she and Mike purchased lifejackets for themselves, too, because they were unwilling to rely on rental equipment for their family's safety.

Over the past five years the Bunin/Yokell family has taken four canoe trips: two to the Boundary Waters, one to Quetico, and one on the lower Green River in Utah. Each time they have found it important to plan a good route and the best time of year for the trip. They experienced excellent weather in the Boundary Waters at the end of August, but on the lower Green River at the end of June, they had an entirely different experience.

In canoeing at the Boundary Waters and Quetico, Jane and Mike's philosophy in choosing a route was somewhat different than Cindy Neely's. Both Jane and Mike prefer circle trips. They gather as much information as they can; then, based on their judgment of what their family can comfortably accomplish, they plan a route. But they still remain flexible. Usually, the itinerary includes a decision day on which they can choose between a longer route or a shorter route back. This is important. If things are going well and everyone feels strong, the choice on decision day will be the longer route. If the weather is bad or things are otherwise not going well, the shorter route may be chosen. On the Bunin/Yokell family's three trips to the Boundary Waters and Quetico, they have always opted for the longer routes.

Flexibility is not so easy to work into a river passage. On the trip they took down the lower Green River to its confluence with the Colorado River, the Bunin/Yokell family found themselves anxiously figuring out a way to modify their trip plan. They had planned to do that trip the summer before but had postponed it a year because of the flooding conditions of the river. As Jane recalls, with two parents' work schedules, the boys' summer camp schedules, and the complex schedules of the other family who planned to join them, cancelling their canoe trip was not done lightly. But the extreme flood conditions that included reports of large trees floating in the river convinced Jane that going on the trip would be taking a silly, unnecessary risk.

The next summer the only time they could coordinate the vacation with their friends was in late June. This was just after the spring flood waters had receded—and was the ideal mosquito breeding time. Jane thought she was prepared. She made large, brightly colored sun hats with elastic chin straps and mosquito netting that hung down to the shoulders. She took along quantities of insect repellent and plenty of mosquito netting for the tents. But even so, Abe suffered a strong reaction to the huge number of bites he received. His entire face swelled up, and he was miserable.

There were some fun times—a large sand bar in the middle of the river was bug free, and the two families spent an entire afternoon there. They had mudball fights and buried each other in the sand. The sand bar, saturated below water level,

"After this photograph, let's dig those paddles in!"
Bunin Family Photo.

will forever be remembered as "jello island."

But the hordes of mosquitoes prevailed in the end. The families paddled hard to reach their destination a day earlier than planned. And they had luck. When they reached the take out, they were able to escape the canyon and mosquitoes because of a ranger station there. The park ranger contacted the outfitter by radio, and he picked them up a day early. Flexibility in their trip plan proved important, especially to Abe.

Over the years, Jane has developed some good ideas on how to prepare for a canoe trip, what food to take, and how to pack. The first thing she does is gather information from all available sources, including friends, printed materials, local guides, and outfitters. She then finds out what permits are required for any parks, wilderness areas, or other public lands they expect to use, and obtains them. She makes sure she has a full set of maps for the trip—waterproof maps showing exactly where portages are located as well as USGS seven and one-half minute topographic maps. Having more than one map may cause confusion, but it may be that only one map is actually correct.

One one occasion in the Boundary Waters, Jane's party had three sets of maps: a recent set from an outfitter, an older set from an outfitter, and a USGS seven and one-half minute topographic set. At the end of a very long day when it was getting dark, each map indicated a different route through extremely dense vegetation to their campsite. In the Boundary Waters, parties camp only at designated campsites for two reasons: (1) they're the only places where camping is allowed, and (2) they're the only comfortable campsites because of the dense vegetation and hilly, glaciated terrain. Everyone was tired and hungry, but rather than thrashing through the undergrowth, the party took a break. Jane fed the boys some high-energy snacks (as it was evident that dinner would be very late), then the adults methodically followed one route after another until they found the one which led to the campsite.

As is often the case when a difficult situation arises, taking a break and making sure everyone has something to eat may ward off a potential emergency. To think clearly, it is important to maintain a reasonable blood sugar level, particularly in cases of potential hypothermia. With children, apparently due to their special physiological requirements, it is especially important to keep their bodies well fueled in order to keep them comfortable and in good spirits.

Of course, food is an important matter on any trip. Jane has found that she plans meals for both mountaineering and canoeing in much the same way. For breakfast her family eats the same foods they have at home. Their favorites are cold cereal or oatmeal with Milkman low-fat (not skim) powdered milk, hard-boiled eggs which will keep for several days, or a special breakfast of bagels with cream cheese, eaten early in the trip before the bagels become too stale. For lunch she plans a main course of crackers and cheese, peanut butter and jelly, canned tuna or sardines, plus special treats. They include sugarless candies, sesame crunches, mixed nuts, giant pretzels, and peanut butter boppers. Favorite dinners include spaghetti and tomato sauce (Jane uses powdered tomato soup instead of a can of tomato paste to make the sauce), macaroni and cheese, and freeze-dried dinners made by Alpine Air and the Mountain High brand of Richmore. Some vegetables such as cabbage and carrots keep well and can be used for salads. She packages all meals in bags that include everything needed for that meal. For example, she packs the required amount of powdered milk for the macaroni and cheese with that dinner as well as the other foods on that menu, from soup to dessert. From her years of mountaineering experience, Jane repackages food for canoe trips whenever that will make the food either lighter or more compact. Some people bring glass peanut butter and jelly containers on canoe trips, but Jane prefers to repackage such foods into the same plastic reusable tubes she uses for backpacking.

Because she and Mike prefer circle trips, they anticipate portaging all their equipment a number of times. Their outings have been as long as six days, and that requires lots of food. They plan and pack for canoe trips like they do for backpacking. One difference is that to keep equipment dry, they use two heavy-duty garbage bags inside each pack. Rather than using duffels, Jane and Mike use internal frame backpacks to carry their equipment. They become somewhat scuffed in canoes, but make portaging so much easier that a small amount of damage is an acceptable trade-off. In keeping with their light/compact equipment philosophy, they carry a Svea or Optimus backpacker's stove for cooking.

Like Cindy Neely, the Bunin/Yokell family has found that the appropriate adult to child ratio is two to one on canoe trips. Mike Yokell's father accompanied them on two of their family trips: one where Mike, Ben, and Stan (Mike's father) comprised their entire party; another where Jane, Mike, and their two sons were joined by Stan and a fifteen-year-old cousin of Mike's. This gave them two adults and one child per canoe.

As this latter trip to the Boundary Waters began, the rule of two adults and one child per canoe was strictly enforced. As the outing progressed, people shifted around and both boys would sometimes be accompanied by only one adult. On the lower Green River trip, their family of four had just one canoe, as did their friends' family of four. On that trip, keeping all gear as well organized and compact as possible was critical.

In choosing friends or relatives to share a vacation, it helps to know them well. Mike's fifteen-year-old cousin, though an adult in size, was still only a teenager. Being from Florida, he found the water too cold to swim in; he found his share of the load almost more than he could carry on portages; the trip was much more rigorous than he had expected. Jane felt he actually suffered at times. Then a few weeks after they returned home they received a wonderful letter from Mike's cousin telling them what a great experience he had had and thanking them. In that case the young cousin did not ruin the trip. Remember, however, that mismatched personalities can adversely affect the experience for everyone.

For relaxing in camp, Jane always packs a deck of cards and some compact portable games including Scrabble, checkers, and chess. The list is endless, however, and depends on what your family prefers.

Although Jane loves clothes made of natural fibers, she chooses clothes made of acrylic, polyester, and polypropylene for canoeing and mountaineering trips. Having long underwear made of polypropylene can be very important on damp, rainy days; and sweatsuits of acrylic dry quickly if they become wet. Good raincoats and rainpants are on Jane's list of critical equipment, as are good sun hats, long-sleeved sun shirts, and sun cream. Her recommendation for the latter is Piz Buin, which, although expensive, goes a long way and doesn't irritate her children's skin.

For a tent the Bunin/Yokell family uses a large four-man expedition type tent. They have smaller tents and could take a combination of them, but prefer the large tent because it provides one place where the whole family can be snug and comfortable together.

Like Cindy Neely, Jane Bunin and Mike Yokell prefer to rent from an outfitter rather than buy their own canoe. Given their full schedules, they usually fly to the put-in rather than drive, which means they can't transport their own canoe. The friends and relatives who they go with don't own canoes either, so an outfitter would be required in any case.

OBSERVATIONS:
And Some Helpful Hints

Canoeing provides an opportunity for families to travel through the wilderness without requiring the adults to carry everyone's equipment everywhere. Here are some tips:

(1) Have at least two adults for every child in a party so that paddling and portaging can be accomplished without excessive individual strain.

(2) Pack food, clothing, and sleeping gear in material as waterproof as possible.

(3) In areas such as the Boundary Waters or Quetico, decide whether you want to set up a base camp or take a circle trip. Your choice will depend on personal inclinations and will influence such things as the type of stoves or musical instruments you carry with you.

(4) Be sure to take mosquito hats and insect repellent, sun hats and sun cream, raincoats and pants, boatshoes, child-sized paddles, and lifejackets. They should be included on all lists of prerequisite equipment.

(5) Take a complete set of maps (in waterproof containers if possible) and know how to read them.

(6) In planning, remember that river trips are sometimes easier than journeys involving a series of portages.

(7) In all cases, gather as much information as possible in advance, plan carefully, and maintain as much flexibility in the trip plan as possible.

(8) Wear lifejackets when in the canoe.

Bicycling near Boulder, Colorado. *Photograph by Vicki DeHaan.*

Chapter Six

Bicycling

B ecause bicycling requires roads or bike paths (we are not concerned about mountain biking here), it is not strictly a wilderness activity. It is, however, an active, adaptable sport that parents can engage in while their children are young.

My family has found that cycling on the bike paths in metropolitan Denver has allowed us to spend time outdoors together for a morning or afternoon without committing the whole day travelling to and from the mountains. Another advantage to cycling is that it may allow families with children of very different ages to participate in a family activity that is fun for all.

The basic requirement is a sturdy bicycle. Next in order are helmets and child seats. Then comes the gear. A small pack strapped behind the child's bicycle seat is large enough to carry boxes of juice, sandwiches, and fruit, as well as sun screen lotion and raingear. It is best to carry a raincoat and pants for the child. Though a poncho is more efficient, it may get caught in the rear wheel.

As for helmets, there are several brands available for children. We opted to purchase a standard size model with an inner band that will adjust to fit Helane's head as she grows.

Helane's helmet is exactly like mine, though at first she was unwilling to put it on. At my parents' suggestion, I discovered that if I put mine on first, she willingly copied me.

There are a number of children's bicycle seats on the market. We chose a heavy plastic model with a high back and armrests that allowed Helane to fall asleep comfortably while riding. The seat belt was adequate to keep her from jumping out, but whenever she fell asleep, we used thick, elastic cords criss-crossed across her chest and under her arms to keep her secure. The child seat worked well during the summers when Helane was two and three years old. Once she turned four, however, her legs were so long that if her feet slipped off the footrest on the child seat, they could have become entangled in the spokes of the rear wheel. She also weighed more than forty pounds, the maximum weight her child seat was manufactured to carry. Another complicating factor was Helane's baby sister Piper. Where do you put the second child? If each one could ride on a parent's bicycle, the answer would be easy. But since Helane was too big to ride in a child seat, and too small to ride her own bike, we had to consider other options.

The one that appeared to make the most sense was a trailer. There are several different models available, each made of various materials. One main consideration in choosing a trailer is whether the children face forward or backward. A second consideration is construction: an aluminum frame covered with nylon fabric versus a roofless molded plastic model. The third consideration is how the trailer will be attached to the bicycle. Some trailers are attached near the seat so that if the bicycle falls over, the trailer also goes over; others are attached near the pedal so that if the bicycle falls over, the trailer remains upright. Of course, by adding a trailer, the bicycle effectively becomes a tricycle and is much less likely to fall over in any case.

Cycling on anything other than separate bicycle paths presents an element of danger, which makes the sport less attractive as a family activity than others discussed in this book. Throughout the country, however, more and more cities, towns, and counties are constructing bicycle paths, thus expanding the possibilities, and many new areas developed for other recreational purposes now include bike paths. Near Denver, for example, the Cherry Creek Reservoir Recreation Area contains many miles of bike paths; another path runs alongside Dillon Reservoir between Frisco and Dillon, Colorado; and one parallels Interstate 70 from Copper Mountain over Vail Pass to Vail.

During the summer when Helane was two, three friends and I bicycled from Frisco to Breckenridge, then to the top of Hoosier Pass. For most of the way from Frisco to Breckenridge there was a newly constructed bike path that paralleled the road. In the sections where there was no path, the shoulders were fairly wide. Because bicyclists travel the road frequently, drivers are aware that they will probably encounter them. I felt that Helane and I were reasonably safe.

After a stop for ice cream in Breckenridge, we continued up the pass. It was a warm summer afternoon and Helane fell asleep. We tied windjackets across her chest to keep her securely in her seat. I fell behind my friends and was not sure whether or not I would make it to the top; so they pedalled on without me. Here I felt rather vulnerable because the shoulders along the road were not always wide, and I was riding alone without other cyclists to draw the attention of motorists.

When we reached the switchbacks near the top, I had to stop riding and walk. Helane remained asleep, which allowed me to keep going. I feared that as soon as she woke up, we would have to turn around. Once the road leveled out, I was able to ride again. Then the top came into sight, and I recognized one of my friends speeding toward us. The other two had ridden down the other side of the pass to Fairplay, where they planned to spend the night. My friend graciously rode back up to the top with me. Helane conveniently awoke when we arrived there and stretched her legs and threw a few snowballs. Even at the age of two, she appreciated the novelty of making snowballs in the middle of July. The ride from the top of the pass all the way down to Frisco was exhilarating! Even though I was unwilling to let go and really speed down the pass as my friend did, Helane thought I lacked caution.

Any time I let go of the brakes, she kicked me and admonished, "Not so fast, Mommy, not so fast."

Friends whose family includes two teenagers as well as two toddlers have discovered that bicycling is the perfect compromise for family sport. When the father pedals along pulling the two toddlers in a trailer, he has had a workout at about the same time that his wife and teenage daughters are ready to call it a day. Their teenagers are often too busy to devote more than half a day to a family outing, and the toddlers become restless after much more than two hours. So they plan two hours of riding to bring them to their picnic spot, then two hours of return riding to complete the excursion. Our friends point out that it is hard to find a movie that appeals to everyone in their family. A bicycle route is easier to locate and much more fun.

OBSERVATIONS:
And Some Helpful Hints

Bicycling is an easy, enjoyable outdoor family activity. Keep these points in mind:

(1) Safety is the main element of concern. Use bicycle helmets, a suitable child seat or trailer, and take a route along a bicycle path or a road with wide shoulders.

(2) Remember to take along thick, elastic cords or extra jackets to secure a sleeping passenger in a child seat.

(3) Take plenty of water or boxes of juice. Passengers seem to get as thirsty as pedalers.

(4) Remember that a park with a playground makes a good objective for a family bicycle outing.

(5) Check around your local area for bike paths in parks, along rivers or canals, or parallel to stretches of highway.

(6) Keep in mind that the great advantage of cycling is that it's possible for all ages to ride or be carried along in a seat or trailer. It can be done anywhere there's a road, and it doesn't take much time.

Epilogue

The greatest difficulty in writing this book was in deciding when to stop writing! Each family I spoke to thought of at least one other family that I should contact, and each had at least one more exciting trip that I should include. Everyone I interviewed inspired me to try a trip such as they had done. I can hardly wait to go canoeing, and we should be able to fit a horsepack trip into this summer's camping schedule.

I hope the information has the same effect on you. All these people take their kids with them into the wilderness, and so can you!

Contributors

Let me introduce the families who contributed to this book:

Betsy and Gene White of Berkeley, California. Both Gene and Betsy have climbed extensively in the Andes and Himalayas as well as throughout the western United States and Canada. Their three children are Eric, born in 1964; Greg, born in 1968; and Laura, born in 1970. Gene and Betsy took all three children on trips into the wilderness from the age of one month. The Whites lived in Pakistan when their oldest son, Eric, was young and he traveled with them in the mountains there. The whole family took a successful trek to the Annapurna Sanctuary in Nepal when the children were ages seven, nine, and thirteen.

Sue Ellen Harrison and Michael McCarthy of Boulder, Colorado. Sue Ellen has been more involved in hiking and backpacking than Michael. Their children are Brooke, born in 1979, and Fenton, born in 1982. They have experienced the transition from cross-country skiing first alone, then with children, to downhill skiing when their children were young.

Barbara and Mike Martin of Denver, Colorado. Friends of Gene and Betsy White, they have been on wilderness trips involving groups of families including the Whites. Barbara and Mike have two sons: Doug, born in 1975, and Neil, born in 1977. Desert backpacking is a favorite vacation of theirs, and they have several spots in Utah and Arizona to which they love to return.

Reola and George McLeod of Denver, Colorado. Both George and Reola have worked for years for Colorado Outward Bound School. George spent seven years in Antarctica and was a member of the 1985 American Everest Expedition. Their sons are Ian, born in 1975, and Scott, born in 1978. Reola has backpacked as the sole adult with both boys while George was climbing the Himalayas.

Maggie and Bob Taylor of Denver, Colorado. Maggie and Bob own a ranch in southern Colorado where their children Marissa, born in 1981, and Sam, born in 1983, both learned to ride horses. Bob has two teenage daughters who live with Maggie and Bob, and they have found that the challenge of finding an outside activity the whole family enjoys has been best met by bicycling.

Debi and Jerry Jung of Littleton, Colorado. Debi and Jerry are formidable "peak baggers." Their sons are Eric, born in 1977; Christopher, born in 1980; and Mickail, born in 1984. By the time Eric was one year old, he had "climbed" twenty-five of Colorado's fourteeners.

Dale Hayes and Bill Bredehoft of Billings, Montana. Formerly of Boston, Dale and Bill have climbed extensively in the eastern United States. Now living in the West with their children, Patrick, born in 1980, and Rebecca, born in 1984, they have begun taking advantage of the climbing opportunities offered by the Rocky Mountains.

Jane Bunin and Mike Yokell of Boulder, Colorado. Both

Jane and Mike are experienced rock climbers and well-seasoned mountaineers. Their sons Benjamin, born in 1976, and Abraham, born in 1980, have been on numerous hikes and backpack trips. When Benjamin was five years old, Mike took him on a canoe trip in the Boundary Waters Wilderness Area. Subsequently, the whole family has canoed together on multi-day trips and horsepacked into the Wind River Mountains in Wyoming.

Jini and John Griffiths of Hailey, Idaho. Jini and John have both worked professionally as mountaineers for Northwest Outward Bound School, and as river guides. Jini reached the summit of Anna Dablam in the Himalayas as a member of the women's expedition of 1983. Their daughter Erin was born in 1984 and cross-country skied many times during her first winter in a wooden toboggan the Griffiths now manufacture commercially.

Cindy Neely of Georgetown, Colorado. Cindy has enjoyed the sport of canoeing for thirty-five years, ever since she herself was a child. She first introduced her son Ted, born in 1963, to the joys of water travel when he was eleven. That proved so successful that she took her younger son, Burr, born in 1974, on his first canoe trip at the age of five.

Barbara Euser and Dean Crowell of Denver, Colorado. Dean and I have both done substantial amounts of hiking and backpacking, I have climbed in the Andes in Colombia, Ecuador, and Peru; and in the Pamirs in the U.S.S.R. Rock climbing was my favorite sport during college and in the five years I was instructor for Colorado Outward Bound School. Since becoming a lawyer, a wife, and a mother of two daughters, Helane, born in October 1981, and Piper, born in June 1985, hiking and cross-country skiing have been my major outdoor activities.

Further Reading

As more and more people have successful family experiences in the wilderness, more and more is written on the subject. Several years ago, Marilyn Doan wrote for the Sierra Club a book entitled *Starting Small in the Wilderness*. She produced an in-depth reference book, particularly in her extremely detailed descriptions of equipment, including patterns and information on how to make your own. If you know nothing about hiking and backpacking, this book will surely tell you all you need to know. My only reservation is that it's a bit overwhelming. It's certainly a valuable source book—but don't let Ms. Doan's attention to every last detail discourage you.

An entirely different type of book, excellent and most interesting, is Joseph Bharat Cornell's *Sharing Nature With Children*. He calls it a parent-teacher nature-awareness guidebook. The book has nothing to do with the mechanics of hiking or backpacking, but everything to do with how you enjoy the wilderness once you get there. Every page is filled with games and other activities to increase parents' and children's appreciation of the fascinating environment to which they have come. Games are identified by mood: calm/reflective; active/observational; or energetic/playful. They are also indexed according to what they teach: attitudes and qualities, concepts, and environment. My response to the book was not only how much I have to teach as a parent, but how much I have to learn as a parent! A third book on the subject of adventuring with children is Maureen Wheeler's *Travel With Children*. Described as a survival kit for travel in Asia, I found that the book had first to do with developing a philosophy of including children in whatever adventures the family undertakes, and, second, to developing the techniques to include children with ease and minimum strain on parents and children. Whether or not one plans to travel in Asia, I found Ms. Wheeler's philosophy and general approach to problem solving worthwhile reading.

I have often come across information on hiking and climbing with children unexpectedly. In *Women on the Rope—The Feminine Share in Mountain Adventure*, Cicely Williams included a chapter entitled "Like Mother, Like Daughter." Reading the chapter, I learned that women mountaineers have included their daughters, sons, and husbands in their climbing; her history of British climbing en famille commences in the 1930s. In the 1950s, Miriam Underhill, an American, climbed in the Alps with her two sons, Bobby and Brian. Introducing the boys to climbing at an early age apparently taught them to love the sport. In the late 1960s, Brian was actively climbing while he was a graduate student at the University of Colorado, and I knew him as a member of the Rocky Mountain Rescue Group. Once again I was impressed by the fact that hiking and climbing with children was certainly feasible, and something that has been done for years. Though sometimes we feel like pioneers, it's reassuring to learn from books like that of Cecily Williams that the real pioneers were successfully doing these things decades ago.

Periodicals also carry informative articles on how to camp, hike, and backpack with children. In the summer of 1985, the June issue of *Outside* magazine included several related articles on introducing children to outdoor sports. In July, *Backpacker* carried an article on children's camping equipment. In March 1986, *Colorado Sports Styles* ran an article oriented to family car camping rather than backpacking, but containing valuable suggestions that apply to any kind of camping involving children. Keep an eye out for this type of article—every parent or author has some interesting tip to offer.

Information on introducing children to the wilderness is easy to obtain from libraries and local bookstores.

Manufacturers and Suppliers of Outdoor Equipment for Children

American Widgeon
4421 20th Street
San Francisco, CA 94114
Outdoor apparel

Baby Bag
138 Hartley Street
Portland, ME 04103
*Quilted fiberfill
bag with divided legs*

Bailen Helmets
2680 Bridgeway
Sausalito, CA 94965
*Adjustable bicycle
helmets*

Bell Helmets
15301 Shoemaker Avenue
P.O. Box 1020 ·
Norwalk, CA 90680
Bicycle helmets

Cannondale Corp.
9 Brookside Place
Georgetown, CT 06829
*Bicycle trailer which
attaches to seat post*

Chuck Roast
Odell Hill Road
Conway, NH 03818
Outdoor apparel

Dolt of California
10455 W. Jefferson Blvd.
Culver City, CA 90230
Daypacks

Eastpak
17 Locust Street
Haverhill, MA 01830
Daypacks

Fabiano Shoe Co., Inc.
850 Summer Street
Boston, MA 02127
Hiking boots

Gerry
6260 Downing
Denver, CO 80216
*Classic aluminum frame
back baby carrier; also
cloth baby front carrier*

Griffiths, Jini and John
P.O. Box 398
Hailey, ID 83333
Child carrier toboggan

Henderson Camp Products
300 W. Washington Street
Chicago, IL 60606
Sleeping bags

Hi-Tech Sports U.S.A., Inc.,
4500 North Star Way
Modesto, CA 95356
Hiking boots

Jan Sport
Jan Sport Building
Paine Field Industrial Park
Everett, WA 98204
Frame packs

Johnson Camping, Inc./
Camp Trails
1 Marine Midland Plaza
P.O. Box 966
Binghamton, NY 13902
Daypacks, frame packs

Karhu-Titan
55 Green Mountain Drive South
Burlington, VT 05401
Cross-country skis

Kastle
P.O. Box 1208
Clearfield, UT 84016
Downhill skis

Kayak Specialties
P.O. Box 152
Buchanan, MI 49107
Lifejackets

Kelty Pack Inc.
P.O. Box 7048-A
St. Louis, MO 63177
Packs, sleeping bags

KinderGear
25545 County Road 56
Steamboat Springs, CO 80487
*Apparel, child-size
snowshoes, child carriers,
toboggans*

L.L. Bean
Casco Street
Freeport, ME 04033
Outdoor apparel

Log House Designs, Inc.
HCR-68 Box 248
Center Conway, NH 03813
Outdoor apparel

Mountain Masters
P.O. Box 1831
Grass Valley, CA 95945
Child backpack carrier

Mountainsmith, Inc.
1100 Simms Street
Golden, CO 80401
Child backpack carrier

The North Face
999 Harrison Street
Berkeley, CA 94710
Child-size sleeping bags

Pacific Mountain Sports
910 Foothill Blvd.
La Canada, CA 91011
Hiking boots

Patagonia, Inc.
P.O. Box 150
259 W. Santa Clara
Ventura, CA 93301
Outdoor apparel

Peak One/The Coleman
Company
250 N. St. Francis
Wichita, KS 67201
Frame packs

Recreational Equipment, Inc.
(R.E.I.)
1525 11th Avenue
P.O. Box 21685
Seattle, WA 98118
Outdoor apparel, packs, tents

Sierra West
6 East Yanalani
Santa Barbara, CA 93101
Outdoor apparel

Snugli
12980 W. Cedar Drive
Lakewood, CO 80228
*Classic cloth front
baby carrier*

Tough Traveler, Ltd.
Geneva Road
Brewster, NY 10509
Child backpack carrier

Troxel
Highway 57 West
Moscow, TN 38057
Bicycle child-carrier seat

Wilderness Experience
20675 Nordhoff Street
Chatsworth, CA 91311
*Outdoor apparel, day
and frame packs*

Index

Other Outdoor Books from Cordillera Press

COLORADO'S OTHER MOUNTAINS:
A Climbing Guide to Selected Peaks Under 14,000 Feet
Walter R. Borneman
Paperback, 160 Pages, Photographs and Maps $8.95

COLORADO'S HIGH THIRTEENERS:
A Climbing & Hiking Guide
Mike Garratt and Bob Martin
Paperback, 264 Pages, 60 Photographs and Maps $12.95

COLORADO'S SAN JUAN MOUNTAINS:
A Climbing & Hiking Guide
Robert F. Rosebrough
Paperback, 280 Pages, 60 Photographs and Maps $12.95

ROOF OF THE ROCKIES:
A History of Colorado Mountaineering
William M. Bueler
(New, revised second edition)
Paperback, 264 Pages, 60 Photographs and Maps $12.95

THE OUTDOOR ATHLETE:
Total Training for Outdoor Performance
Steve Ilg
Paperback, 250 Pages, 75 Photographs $11.95
(Fall 1987)

ARIZONA'S MOUNTAINS:
A Hiking & Climbing Guide
Bob and Dotty Martin
Paperback, 200 Pages, Photos $11.95
(Fall 1987)

For additional information, call or write:

CORDILLERA PRESS, INC.
Post Office Box 3699
Evergreen, Colorado 80439
(303) 670-3010